UNHISTORIC ACTS

INSIDE THE WOMEN'S MOVEMENT ON PRINCE EDWARD ISLAND

"*Unhistoric Acts* documents Dianne Porter's remarkable life — a life characterized by commitment, determination, and courage. Whether behind the scenes or front and centre, Dianne has always found ways to collaborate with disparate groups and individuals on a common purpose — to improve the lives of Island women and their families. In *Unhistoric Acts*, Dianne turns the spotlight on the women who have played a pivotal role in advancing gender equality in Prince Edward Island."

—Dr. Katherine Arnup, PhD
Author of *'I don't have time for this!' A Compassionate Guide to Caring for Your Parents and Yourself.*

"Dianne Porter provides a rare glimpse into the history of the women's movement in PEI from a personal perspective of one who was immersed in advocating for issues of social justice, equity, and family supports. Her own experiences are woven through the reflections of her colleagues and friends who – as "unsung heroes" – have influenced life as we know it in PEI in the 21st century."

—Kathleen Flanagan,
PhD Candidate
Lifelong Childhood Education Specialist

"Dianne Porter's focus on sharing her own experience in the feminist movement, while amplifying the voices of the others, is inspiring. Her book is an important account of how Island life has been transformed by the people, the policy work, and the advocacy that has led to where we are today."

—Sara Roach Lewis
Author of *She Rules: What You Didn't Know is Holding You Back in Business*

UNHISTORIC ACTS

Inside the Women's Movement
on Prince Edward Island

DIANNE PORTER

pownal
street
press

CHARLOTTETOWN
PRINCE EDWARD ISLAND

pownal
street
press

www.pownalstreetpress.com

DEDICATION

This book is for my life partner, my late husband, Dr. Peter J. Porter.

From the time we met, his encouragement was steadfast, which gave me the freedom to follow my own path rather than to stay on the doorstep.

A meditation labyrinth at the Charlottetown Provincial Palliative Care Center has been built in Peter's memory.

"Walking a labyrinth clears the mind and gives insight into the spiritual journey. It urges action. It calms people in the throes of life transitions. It helps them see their lives in a context of a path, a pilgrimage. They realize that they are not human beings on a spiritual path but spiritual beings on a human path."

From *Walking a Sacred Path* by Lauren Artress

Table of Contents

"The growing good of the world is partly dependent on unhistoric acts; and that things are not so ill with you and me as they might have been, is half owing to the number who lived faithfully a hidden life, and rest in unvisited tombs."

—George Eliot, *Middlemarch*

Introduction: The Labyrinth

The following are chapters based on selected equality issues and activities during my lifetime. These chapters begin in early childhood and end in my senior years. I describe my activities, through my own eyes, and from a position of experience, as I travelled through my young adult life and early motherhood. I began my fifty years on Prince Edward Island working in the dental profession, alongside my husband, Peter.

I have worked collaboratively with many other women who have dedicated their time, knowledge and expertise to the fight for women's equality on Prince Edward Island. Along with my own story, I have also included their stories — of bravery, of challenge, and of success. These women deserve to be recognized, as they are the unsung heroes of the Prince Edward Island women's movement. In most cases, they partnered in the work, with their boots on the ground, and they are worthy of the celebration; they took what seemed to be impossible and just made it happen. I am happy to honour their stories here.

I have always been willing to question, examine the angles, and then express my values. I should note that I have not wished to replace the male view, but only to complement it. My goal, for many years, has been to change the blindness of male chauvinism to include women's perspectives, their lives and priorities, and to give us both a chance to become better, to share the burden, and to be true to our time. It has not been an easy path, but when I see the world my granddaughters will grow up in, I know we have made great strides.

To break the silence of women's voices is an act of love. I don't pretend to have all the answers, I did not invent history and I can't explain its logic with reason alone. I am always questioning, seeking knowledge and then using a sometimes emotional platform to express my opinion. Intellectualism alone is stark and bare.

I have wanted to be one of the voices for those who stand unsheltered by the system — the crazy people of the world who dare to believe in equity and solidarity with a commitment to the future. I dream big dreams and many women I have met on this labyrinth's path do also, and this we must continue. It is important to me to write about the necessary changes that take women from their knees; to see them rise up after so many humiliating years has brought me such joy. I write the secret, forbidden history that is still alive. With this work, I hope to override paternalistic and patriarchal world views, and the single-mindedness that comes with them. My expression of these feelings has always been difficult, but putting those hidden feelings and thoughts into words is my goal.

I try to write so people will love each other more, even if it takes the next generation to get things done. I take the long view, so my solutions and promotions may be at odds with those who like to patch things up now and only work with other women. Choosing to work jointly with both men and women to achieve the goals guaranteed in the Canadian Charter of Rights and Freedoms has been my strategy. I believe change happens in small, poetic moments and if you miss an opportunity to change a mind or a direction of an argument or a policy, you may never get a second chance.

The labyrinth is a symbol of the path I have followed and it is a two way street. Studying the labyrinth is to learn to walk a pathway where every person does so at their own speed, in their own time and in their own way. This book demonstrates the pathway I have taken in life, which was never a straight line nor an easy journey. In trusting the path, I hoped it would take me to my own centre — and it has.

The women I have known and worked with are the unsung heroes in this book, and each has travelled at their own pace. They made it possible for me to walk with them towards equality, but at times we all walk alone into our own issues and places of challenge. Most of the time, my rule of thumb has been to sidestep around the barricades without disturbing others, but as in life, there have been times when the doors needed to be kicked in. All travelling in our own way, we have taken turns being comfortable with the status quo, letting others step up to take the lead when we cannot until we are strong enough to fight again. Women in our group have come and gone, walked alone, joined other movements, and returned. It has always been our premise to accommodate one another, to accept all at their own pace.

I have had the privilege of listening to the life experience of many individuals, and worked with many women since I was first introduced to the labyrinth, this symbol of wholeness. I have adopted this as a way to share some of my experiences, and as this memoir progresses and I plot my life journey as a feminist, I am proud to say that I have walked most of this journey with these extraordinary Island women.

While studying at Carleton University in Ottawa, I often spent time browsing in the women's bookstore on Bank Street, and checked out the bulletin board looking for extracurricular activities in the area where I lived. On one such day, I was drawn to a small notice of a new reading group being formed. The goal was to study selected stories from Clarissa Pinkola Estés' book, *Women Who Run With the Wolves*, whose basic tenet is that within every woman there lives a powerful internal force — filled with instincts, passionate creativity, and ageless knowing. At our first gathering, the symbol of the labyrinth was introduced as a pathway for our study and for our lives. In my lifetime there have been times of change when it was difficult to see the path ahead. I have paused at the turns and questioned. Other times, I had a deep feeling of trust and I kept on going, even though I did not know just what was ahead for me.

Women in Prince Edward Island have joined forces to create change for generations. This book highlights my fifty-year journey of working on equality issues on Prince Edward Island, and with my co-pilots the unsung heroes, today we celebrate the long road we have walked together.

Chapter One:
The girl who said no

Feminism is defined as a range of social movements and ideologies that aim to define the political, economic, personal, and social equality of the sexes. Feminism incorporates the position that societies prioritise the male point of view, and that women are treated unjustly, their voices even undervalued. In my life, I have worked as a feminist; I have never been satisfied with being silent or invisible. Looking back, it is easy to define the pivotal moments where I resisted stereotyping and fought against injustice — and as Robert Frost says of the road, "I took the one less travelled by, and that has made all the difference." Those times of resistance indeed developed my character.

I've always been a feminist; there is a pattern in my life journey and I have trusted this path. I have learned to see in the darkness of life and find a way out, not just for myself but for others as well. Being a feminist is not for the faint of heart, but while it has indeed been fraught with difficulty, sometimes excruciatingly so, it has also been dotted with satisfaction, love, and joyful celebration.

While studying the genealogy of my family, I learned that I am a seventh generation Canadian. The Hogg family members were colonists in British North America, settling as a military family in New York State. They became known as Loyalists when, after the American Revolutionary War, they left America and settled in Nova Scotia's Shelburne, the capital at the time. The year was 1783, shortly after the American Declaration

Mum and Dad, 1957

of Independence. The Harris side of the family arrived nearly a century later as immigrants from Wales and settled in rural Shelburne County as farmers.

The marriage of my maternal grandparents, Harold K. Hogg and Katie V. Harris, brought the two families together in 1904. Shortly after their marriage, they moved to Windsor, Nova Scotia where the family attended Saint John Presbyterian Church, and my grandfather was a harness maker. Windsor is where my mother, Gladys Olga Hogg, was born, and where she gave birth to me in 1949. She and Robert N. Swindall were my parents. I was four years old when they separated, after a difficult marriage rife with violence, harsh words, and abuse against my mother. Later, my stepfather, Herman E. Whitehead, became not only my mother's spouse, but Dad — the father of two step-siblings. He still resides in Nova Scotia. My mother died of old age in 2021.

She leaves behind a heap of children. My sister, Carol, was the oldest and was given much responsibility, including making meals for myself and the other children. My younger sister Maggie lives here in Charlottetown,

Siblings, 1957. Back row: Maggie, Carol, Dianne; front row: David, Alice, Mary

PEI, and as a child spent her days helping with the neighbours' horses for a chance to take one for a ride. Mary is currently retired, a modern senior nomad who has set out to travel the world as much as possible in an RV. Alice lives near Peggy's Cove, Nova Scotia, and the only brother, David, lives about fifty feet from where our childhood home once stood in Windsor.

I never really understood the impact that I had on my younger siblings at the time, but now when we sit together as a family we share stories from childhood. We all agree, it could have been a lot less stressful if we had a better house, or if our parents had better jobs. Like all large families, everyone had a role to play in looking after one another. We were always aware that Carol, who had the after-school responsibility of starting supper, had been given a big job. Often, some of us would join in to peel the potatoes, and another would walk to the farm up the hill to get the eggs or milk.

One of my younger sisters, Mary, once told me how grateful she was for having me comb her hair every day before school and find her clothes to put on. She even remembers the time when I found her a dress for the high school graduation dance. Honestly, I don't remember much of those days. It was simply part of my life; I offered care and comfort to my younger siblings. Alice adds that yes, while I did indeed brush her hair every morning, what has stayed with her is the feeling of the cold, wet face cloth as I wiped the morning's breakfast off her face before she ran out the door to school. Sister Maggie was always the last out of bed and I'm sure the school bus for high school waited for her more than once. My brother, David, tells stories of being overwhelmed by the five girls. He says he was pretty intimidated by us telling him what to wear, and how to comb his beautiful blonde hair. One year, he even shaved his head to cut the comments — horrifying us all in the process of course.

In elementary school I was known as someone who fought against injustice. In grade three we had a teacher who systematically lined up some of the class randomly for "a taste of the strap". The strap was a wide piece of leather about a foot long and three inches wide, standard issue from the school board. My teacher, an angry old man, was a retired minister recruited to teach the ever-expanding baby boom generation when real teachers were in short supply, and he used fear as a motivator. I felt helpless in these situations. It went on for months, and regularly someone broke down crying. The tension in the class was high.

On one particular day I was called upon to come to the front for "my turn". I stood on the tips of my toes and said "NO!" In a rage of fury, I ran out of the classroom, right past the coat rack and out the back door and headed madly for home. Even though it was February, I didn't feel the cold, as I kept running the whole two miles home. When I arrived at the house, Mum was doing the laundry with the old wringer-washer, and she was startled to see me flying in the back door. Since we didn't have a phone in those days, she had no idea that one of her flock had flown the coop. When she held me I felt safe, and she dried my tears and listened to me, gradually getting the whole story. She marched over to the neighbour's house to use the phone and called for a taxi, and soon the two of us headed back to the school.

Sitting on a chair in the principal's office, I blurted out the injustice of this corporal punishment, suggesting there must be a better way. I was

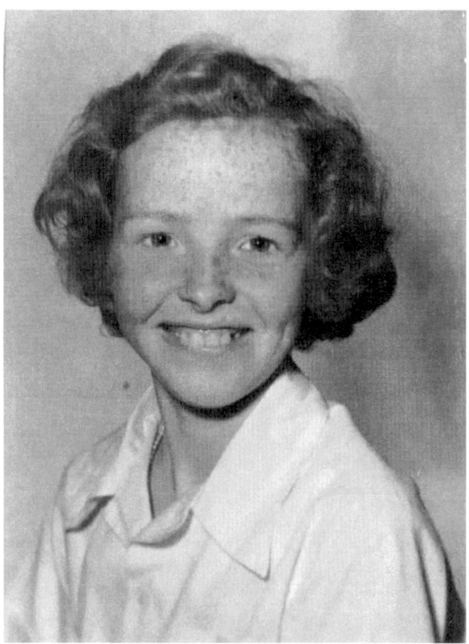

Dianne, 1957, age 8

given candy and left alone in the principal's office, while they went to discuss the problem with the teacher. On their return, it was agreed upon that I could stay home for the rest of the week because I was upset. I was to return to school the following Monday.

When Monday arrived I noticed a big change in how I was being treated by the kids on the playground. They gathered to ask, "Why did you run home?" "Why did you go without your coat?" and, " What happened after that?" This is when I officially became known as *The Girl Who Said No*. The positive effect should be noted: that was the last time any child was strapped or threatened with one in my classroom.

Although I was a town girl, I spent many summers on farms owned by aunts and uncles where I accomplished chores and had new experiences. We chased garter snakes through newly-raked hay fields, helped with the separator that skimmed the milk for the cream for the local dairy and made up games to play on Sundays, when our usual games were forbidden. Aunt Katie had been a missionary during the 1940s, and when I was visiting with her, we rang the bell for church each Sunday. Those memories of childhood summers reflect the simple rural summer joys of a townie in the country.

Sandra, Dianne and Barbara; high school
friends from Windsor, Nova Scotia

The roots run deep in my home community, and many of my friends from Windsor are still friends today. My two best high school friends, Sandra and Barbara, were cheerleaders like me, and we all had red hair and lived on the same road. We went to school together, and often shopped together, travelling to Halifax on the Dayliner and back home at suppertime. We had sleepovers, enjoyed our teen years with the Beatles at high school parties, and attended the coffeehouse set up by parents in the United Church basement. On Saturday nights we went to the Windsor Community Centre for the weekly rock and roll dances.

Barbara's mother died when we were young teens, so going to Barb's house after school and helping was as natural as if she was in my own family. There were other friends from high school, but Barbara and Sandra remain life-long friends.

During the school year, my local babysitting paid for my pantyhose and a trip to Walker's restaurant for a coke and french fries, where we watched the boys from Kings College School, a private boy's school in town. One frequent babysitting job was with the Windsor's school superintendent's family. When I was in grade twelve he asked if I would teach in one of the rural schools after graduation and take teacher training in the summer months. For me, however, part of growing up meant leaving home, so instead I packed up a small trunk and headed for Halifax to look for a job after graduation. Mother's wish was that I become a dietitian; after all, I had won the graduation prize in Home Economics.

My mother and I had a great relationship and kept in touch regularly no matter where I was living. Her calls were short, factual and all business. It was like we were back to the times when party lines existed and callers needed to keep the lines free for others. On the day before my mother died in 2021 she called, and talked and talked and talked. We covered many topics from grandchildren to politics and the weather. Looking back I can see that it was her goodbye call because the next morning — she was gone.

After high school, when I lived in Halifax, I got to know young people from all over the province who were working in the city. One of my housemates was from Guysborough County, and worked as a dental assistant. She influenced my decision to enter this training. I secured a Canada Student Loan, a fairly new program at the time, and applied for a spot at the Nova Scotia Institute of Technology. There was a month during that year of training when a gap grew between the student loan and the arrival of a bursary so I slept on the sofa of one of my Windsor friends, Barbara. Newly married and a new parent, she and John gave me a place to call home for a month.

As part of the dental assistant training, our class completed a practicum at the Dalhousie University Dental School Clinic and we were evaluated by both clinic staff and the dental students we were assigned to work with. Towards the end of this block of training I was assigned to Peter Porter, a fourth year dental student. We worked together for several weeks and got to know one another while treating the patients, most of whom were children. Mostly, I kept the dental unit organized, managed the suctioning during dental procedures, and tried to keep the children calm. I mixed dental filling material and went for supplies from the clinic dispensary. The women there, the older dental assistants, were great teachers.

Shortly after my training with Peter ended and when the evaluation was completed, Peter asked me out on a date. I was startled at first since the thought running through my mind was, *how can someone older than me and that kind, not be married?* But I gave him my phone number and asked him to call me. After he left the clinic, I immediately spoke with the women in the dispensary and found out about his life as a student. Our first dates were later that week and from then on, we were a couple. It felt right immediately, so we dated for about two years and then got married in 1973. When he died in 2018 we had been married for forty-five years.

CHAPTER TWO:
EARLY LEADERSHIP

Following graduation in 1971, I moved to Prince Edward Island for my first dental assistant job. I had met Dr. G. Barrett at the Dalhousie Dental Clinic where he offered me the job. When I arrived in Prince Edward Island, I was twenty-one years old, and I became the first formally-trained dental assistant in the province.

Moving to the Island was one of the best decisions we ever made. Peter worked with the children's dental program and was headquartered in Summerside, where he lived and travelled throughout Prince County in a mobile dental clinic. I lived and worked in Charlottetown, and our courtship was a weekend relationship of road trips around the Island. We fell in love *on* the Island and *with* the Island at the same time — and even back then, we knew we would be here forever.

The year I arrived was the first year that Holland College was starting to educate and train dental assistants. They asked if I could help in the evenings to deliver an upgrading program for dental assistants who were already working in dental offices, but who did not hold any qualifying credentials. The next thing I knew, I was hired as a full-time instructor. Holland College follows a unique method for educating and training students. The Developing a Curriculum style of education, (DACUM) pioneered at Ohio State, a system which was brought to the Island by the former college President Dr. Don Glendenning, involves experts in community groups being brought in to advise and develop the objectives

Dianne, Dental Assistant, 1971

of a particular program. In this system, students follow a "Self Teaching and Evaluation Program" (STEP). Students then follow the objectives accepted as the industry standard approved and accredited by the Canadian Dental Association. Part of my job as an instructor was to prepare learning materials, to provide specific objectives, and to conduct evaluations, both for individuals and also small groups. Learning this DACUM system was also great training for me to continue my own education, which was very rewarding.

After Peter and I married, we headed out west as newlyweds. Our honeymoon was a northern drive around Lake Superior, and across Canada to Winnipeg where we spent three years. Peter was a graduate student studying orthodontics at the University of Manitoba, and I taught at Red River Community College (RRCC), in their new Dental Assistant program. Iris Gold was a dental hygienist and also the program Director. Her focus was on the basic health sciences, and my job was to develop and deliver the clinical and laboratory programs.

When I first arrived, the clinic room was empty and there was a list of sixty students who were set to arrive in two weeks. I flew into overdrive with a list of dentists in one hand and a list of needed supplies and equipment in the other. I called on dozens of city dentists, who agreed to donate some supplies and lend me some larger items. After dropping into the offices to gather it all, I made a stop at the University of Manitoba where I spoke with the Dental School Clinic's leadership, the staff dental assistants, and the women in the clinic dispensary. With well wishes and more donated items, I set up the first makeshift dental laboratory at RRCC, which was used for medical laboratory technicians part-time. I was able to put together a few trays of common dental instruments for simple procedures, to introduce the students to the basics as a starting point. The students arrived — but their textbooks didn't. For the whole first month, then, they had to go without. The students studied the handouts and photocopies from the Nova Scotia and Holland College training programs. By the next fall our clinic, the lab, and my nearby office were finished, complete with instruments, manuals, and a full complement of programming. With my sixty students, my claim to fame was to always call them each by name at the beginning of the second class. In the first class I had them introduce themselves to one another. In Manitoba this was a major challenge for me because there were no MacDonalds or Smiths, the Maritime names I was familiar with. Manitoba has a large diverse population so I was faced with memorizing the names of Indigenous, Ukrainian, and Jewish students as well. For a girl from the Maritimes, this was quite the challenge. As is the habit of most students, they sat in the same spots the next day so naming all of them took a while but was relatively easy. Although my pronunciation might have been a bit off, we had lots of laughs as our group bonded over new names.

Since we had a new program, there was lots of preparation to do before each class. I used the Holland College skill-based program as a starting place for the course, and the Manitoba licensing authority had approved additional dental skills to be taught in the program because the province had been experiencing a shortage of dentists. The scope of practice for our RRCC students was for more intra-oral practice and developing this part of the program, in conjunction with Iris Gold, was a new venture. I had visited the four western Canada dental assistant programs who had expanded programs in order to better understand the integration of assisting and clinical practice. By late Spring when the program was finalized we had moved to a small clinic at the University of Manitoba Dental School to complete the clinical training with volunteer patients. Seeing the project come to fruition was a gratifying experience all around, and although I had no idea at the time, I was getting valuable training in how to be thrifty, rally the troops, and complete a mission with no resources.

At the end of year two, we were evaluated by the Canadian Dental Association with in-person visits, reviews of texts, manuals, facilities, and staffing before were granted accreditation. We welcomed a second dental assistant, Armenia Evaristo, to assist me in the laboratory and clinic with our sixty students. This change alone opened up time for students to pursue skills more independently and receive evaluations at their own rate, a quicker pace for some and slower for those who required more time. With the accredited program in the balance, the College granted more funds for new hires. We added my laboratory assistant, and several hygienists were given contracts to work with us during the clinical part of the program at the University of Manitoba Dental School.

I worked with some wonderful people at the RRCC Health Sciences Department who taught me about operations and management. This included requisitioning supplies, scheduling for the college publications, hiring contract staff, and furthering program development. Also, as part of my employment I was required to enlist in the college's professional development program for instructors. This meant that evenings and college breaks were also busy times for me, requiring study and attention. For new educational concepts and further practices in the dental realm, the education was very helpful.

Forty years later, in 2019, I hosted RRCC's program director, Armenia Evaristo, in PEI. She brought me up to date on the success of the University of Manitoba program throughout her years of working at RRCC. While industry standards are always being updated at the College, the framework and the quality skills-based approach we established in the 1970s is still in use for the accredited program.

Following graduation from the University of Manitoba in 1976, Peter set up an orthodontic practice working part-time in Charlottetown, in hopes that it would eventually become full time. As his graduation gift, I prepared a staff training manual in orthodontics for his dental assistants, since there was no such training at Holland College at the time. Peter was also working as an orthodontics professor at the Dalhousie University Dental School and as the consulting orthodontist with the team at the IWK Children's Hospital with the cleft lip and palate clinic, which meant his days were full. We moved to Halifax in 1976 with our newborn son, Alex. Twice a month, Peter travelled back and forth to provide orthodontic treatment to patients in a tiny Charlottetown office. During our time in Halifax, I became supervisor to dental assistant students from PEI's Holland College, who were completing their practicums at the Dalhousie Dental School Clinic. I also consulted with the Nova Scotia Dental Association on a newly "expanded scope of practice" program for dental assistants in that province. Eventually I was asked by the Canadian Dental Association to be on the Dental Assistant Accreditation Team, which carried out training program evaluations all across the country. This was a demanding role, as it required a lot of pre-visit reviewing of learning materials with post-inspection evaluation reports to write. However, I enjoyed the role for many years. This is where I started to learn to juggle: home, work, and volunteering.

Once we moved back to the Island full time, I managed Peter's Charlottetown orthodontic practice through the Alanem Management Company, which we had set up. Peter always said, "Just put $200 dollars in my bank account each week, and you look after the rest." I became the CFO at the office, managing and supervising staff. Because I was a dental assistant, I was not going to be party to paying the staff the going PEI rate, which I felt was below the Canadian industry standard. There was a bit of push-back from the dental community, but we were glad we held to the principle and paid our staff a higher wage. With the orthodontic training manual for the staff, we trained dental assistants and then coached them in orthodontics on the job. We worked with most of that original group of staff for thirty-eight years and they felt like family. Our point was to invest in people so they would invest, long term, in our practice. We believed it was a successful strategy, and it ensured that quality standards were always front and centre in our practice.

Dentistry on the Island was a family affair; many dentists had spouses who worked with them. Some women were nurses who changed gears to work in the dental clinics, some acted as receptionists and many others were bookkeepers or did the laboratory work. Gradually, over the years we hired and trained additional staff to take on some of my management duties to free up some time for an ever-growing family, but I maintained the supervisory role for those delegated duties. We eagerly adopted computers when they became available and it simplified the office work even further. As manager during the life of the practice, I continually looked to improve the system and gladly welcomed innovations as they occurred. There were daily discussions with Peter about how to improve the practice — including the best ways to deal with the never-ending wait list, procurement of supplies and staffing issues, in addition to reconciling bank statements and paying tax bills. While Peter treated many adults in the practice, he had a real affinity with the children and thereby took a child-centred approach to their treatment. Every decision was to be made based on what was best for the child and he really enjoyed talking to them: he remembered their names, the sports they played, the names of their family members and their favourite professional sports teams.

Peter accommodated the different needs of the patients. In one instance, he discarded boxes of mouthwash that contained alcohol since some of his patients were Muslim and could not use it for post-treatment rinses. He placed a refreshment refrigerator in the waiting room for teen patients who came to the office between classes. Keeping up-to-date, new reading material for children and youth and their parents in the reception room was also a priority so that if the schedule got behind, there were interesting magazines to read.

A few years after the start of the practice, in our second, larger location on Pownal Street in Charlottetown, we hired a practice management consultant to review the patient flow and staff positions to make the expanded office and staff more efficient. From then onward, we followed "quality management" principles which were something new in those days. The front desk improvements were put in place for better scheduling, staff were added in the clinic, and further delegation of the dental assistant's duties were approved to better facilitate the flow of patients. The entire goal was to try to improve the waiting list for treatment. Peter also agreed to delegate part of his clinical orthodontic responsibility to our orthodontics-trained staff. At the office I called him Peter Porter Perfect. Not only was he meticulous in his treatment of orthodontic cases, he also did not deviate from a procedure once he had developed a successful technique, so delegating was difficult for him, and sometimes did not save time because he consistently double checked the staff's work. I often joked, "He makes a great orthodontist, but just try doing the dishes with him at home."

One fact that is seldom spoken of in public among dentists is the extent of their pro bono work. For Peter, he had a pattern to this work. Once he saw a debilitating oral malocclusion and he set up a treatment plan and began the process which could last two to three years. From the outset parents were given a financial plan as well. As treatment progressed so did the payment plan, but for some children there were missed payments at no fault of theirs. Treatment continued and was completed in spite of the non-payment. There were some patients who came back years later and settled a long outstanding balance, much to Peter's surprise. Still others were never given a financial plan and were treated at no cost. No matter their ability to pay, patients received the same excellent care day after day.

After the clinic day, Peter would often have young general dentists stop into the office with an orthodontic case they were having trouble with. GPs could do orthodontics but they were limited in scope. In the best interest of the child, Peter spent his free time coaching GPs in the treatments they were offering to their patients. Orthodontists from the other Atlantic provinces frowned on this mentorship, but it didn't change Peter's commitment to children's orthodontics.

One person who began teaching during the waning part of my time in a teaching career with dental assistants, was in the first graduating class at Holland College, and who soon became a highly respected educator and instructor, was Gaylene Smith. She had worked in Summerside dental offices for nearly five years following graduation and then returned to Holland College to become an educator. When I no longer felt up-to-date on dental assistant education, I encouraged her to take my place to serve with the Canadian Dental Association's accreditation survey team

UNSUNG HERO
GAYLENE SMITH

In 1972, I was in the first graduating class of dental assistants at Holland College and was employed in Summerside before returning to the college as the Program manager, where I remained in the position for twenty three years. Within Holland College I was then promoted as the Coordinator of Health Sciences with a teaching role in the dental assistant program until 2004. I was blessed that the belief at the college for management  was "show us the proof that you can do it". I had tremendous support and opportunities during my twenty-eight years there, where I developed the small program into a respected department that could serve regional students. Luckily, the college was very supportive of the necessary investment in equipment as we grew.

With the recommendation of my predecessor, Dianne Porter, I was appointed to the Canadian Dental Association accreditation team evaluating various training programs across Canada for my whole career. This position required that I travel and observe students, do in-depth reviews of training materials, and complete follow-up communication with students and staff of most dental assistant training programs in Canada. With this high profile in the dental community, our Holland College program became a centre of excellence and consultations with other programs were a normal occurrence.

In 1991, I was approached by the Ontario Dental Association about the advanced scope of practice we taught at the college, and I happily spent time over many years offering short training programs for other dental assistant programs so their students could pursue the advanced skills we taught at Holland College. Because of this work, in 1993 I received a leadership award from the Association of Canadian Community Colleges. Improvements in the Holland College Dental Assistant program were continuous as new materials, procedures, and research became available and allowed us to keep our accreditation status.

Upon my retirement from Holland College, I took a job at the College of the North Atlantic in Newfoundland to assist in the development of a dental assisting program in Doha, Qatar. I developed curriculum, taught students, and led the program in a position that I stayed in for five years. The program in Qatar followed the standards of the Canadian Dental Association accreditation program.

Since retiring, I have been involved with the Mikinduri Children of Hope (MCOH), a non-profit charity who I visited in Kenya with twice to work in a dental clinic that performed 500 tooth removals per day between the three dentists who were part of the visit. It was the only service we could offer to remove the patient's pain. One of the other rewarding actions performed by the charity was the sponsorship of girls to attend school. One of the projects I took on in a leadership role was the collection of sanitary supplies for girls, since it was normal for girls to bargain for these items. At times it meant trading sexual favours with exploitative teachers. With the Vernon River Women's Institute, 2100 reusable sanitary kits were made to distribute to the girls in Mikinduri.

Very close to my heart is the volunteer time I spent with palliative care patients, where I knew that I was making a difference in their lives and where nothing was expected in return.

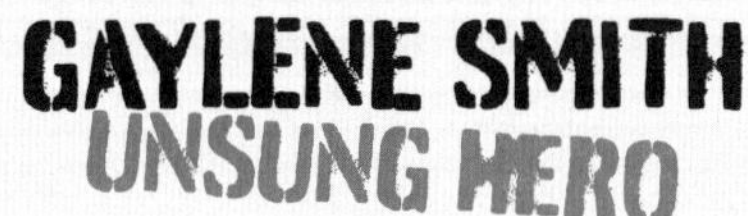

as the dental assistant member, since Holland College remained a high quality program and her teaching and administration skill was excellent. She tells the story of being invited to my home for an encouraging coffee break where I suggested that she take my place on the team. The Canadian Dental Association sets the national quality standards and Gaylene spent more than thirty years both leading the excellent Holland College program and working with the accreditation team. Gaylene would often call on me to come to the college to teach some of the courses she didn't particularly like to teach, and I didn't take a salary for those classes and asked that the funds go towards a bursary program for needy students. Gaylene assures me that the bursary is still awarded annually and my salary was just the beginning.

Peter and I both enjoyed an expanding family life and a challenging work life, along with community involvement and volunteering. There was a natural integration as we made PEI our home. Like most parents we were involved in many activities with the children: soccer, hockey, Brownies, Scouts, gymnastics, and skiing. At the end of the 1970's we had three children: Alex, born in Winnipeg in 1975, Andrea, born in Halifax in 1977, and Emily, born on the Island in 1979.

Peter became actively involved in the dental community, both in the professional association and with a small study club. The study club members became his lifelong friends. One club member, a PEI oral-maxillo-facial surgeon named Dr. Sam Habbi, was someone who became Peter's treatment collaborator regarding surgical patients and also a close personal friend. Our families spent time together and our children all became good friends; in fact, it felt like we were all part of the same extended family. When the children were young, every evening at 6 pm Sam called to arrange a meeting time so he and Peter could spend a few evening hours on orthodontic/surgery case management. They met either at Sam's kitchen table or ours, or in the lab in Sam's office. Amongst our friends they were teased about shopping the sales together looking for the best prices on paper goods for their offices. For many years, when patients were having their surgery at the hospital, Dr. George Saunders assisted Dr. Habbi in the operating room at the Queen Elizabeth Hospital. The Saunders family lived close to our home and the family became close personal friends also. Peter was very sensitive to the fact that surgery is painful, and he empathized with the patients while they were in hospital. It became the standard practice for him to order flowers for each patient during their recovery.

Having three children and working in the orthodontic practice, I juggled the work hours between drop off and pick up at school, kin-

Family photo, Christmas, 1980

dergarten, gymnastics, or hockey. When the children were babies, I carried the books in a box so I could transport them between the dental office and the home office. I did a bit here and a bit there while dealing with the children's schedules. On the day Emily was born, I had Peter bring me that box and set it up on the bedside table in my room at the hospital, because the next day was pay day for the staff.

The accountant was reviewing the finances at tax time that year and he asked, "Why did you not apply for maternity benefits?" I still laugh thinking about that, wondering when I would ever have time to take a leave and do that. For many of the preschool years a woman named Nellie Malone arrived on Tuesdays and Thursdays so I could focus on the orthodontic practice full time on those days. The chaos of looking after things was not unlike many other women I knew: scheduling, arranging, car-pooling, house work, shopping, and meals. Along with the office work, I became a good juggler.

Our family times were busy, but we always managed to gather at suppertime most days to catch up with everyone, make future plans, and to talk Island politics. We debated almost every current event and it became a time of teaching and listening for both Peter and I. During the 1990s I was doing less volunteering but studying at the University of Prince Edward Island, arranging my classes around the children's schedules and making a point of being at home when school was out for the day. I know I was very privileged to be able to create a workable schedule that was a win for the family, a win for the orthodontic practice, and a win for my educational pursuits. I often had evening classes and Peter took over the evening routines, the supervision of homework, the laundry, and getting everyone to bed on time. As a part-time student it took me seven years of study to complete a BA in Political Studies with a minor in Women's Studies and a Diploma in Public Administration. In many ways, in some of the classes it felt like I was getting credit for what I already had learned. The new challenge was the knowledge of political theory.

In the first years of living on PEI, I began looking for early childhood educational programs for the children. The children attended a part-day program a few days a week during the school year at the Basilica Recreation Centre in Charlottetown with Chrystyna Holman, and later with Alice Taylor and then Ann Francis who were all early childhood educators. The children attended half days when they were ages three and four, and then attended half-day, private kindergarten at age five with Mrs. Chang at a local church.

When Emily, my youngest child, was born in 1979, I was appointed by Premier James Lee as the parent representative to the PEI Child Care Facilities Board because I was interested in expanding and improving child care and early childhood programs for the Island's children and their families. Premier Lee also added new elements to the existing Child Care Subsidy program when he became Premier. Under the new child care legislation, the province was required to appoint a parent to be on the Board under the Child Care Facilities Act. I served in this role for seven years. I remember a poster from that time that said, *I wanted to go out and change the world but I couldn't find a babysitter.* This summed up my experience, and the plight of many Island women in the late part of the twentieth century.

Chapter Three:
A New Constitution for Childcare

The chronology of Canadian child care began during the Second World War, when there were labour shortages and consequently women became catapulted into the necessary workforce. Ironically, though, when the war ended, the child care system closed and women were given monthly family allowances; these baby bonuses were meant as a driver to go home, give birth, and replenish the population. But women's insatiable thirst for independence would never be turned around. From the 1940s to today, women in this country lobbied for its citizens — its women — to care about their equality rights, their families, and especially to fight for services to support their children.

Like all young families, child care was an issue for us and trying to piece together a plan that would work was difficult at times. Peter often adjusted his hours around school start times and the children loved having their dad involved with the chaos at the beginning of the school day.

As more women entered the workforce in Prince Edward Island in the 1980s, essential child care became more and more of a necessity. However, there was an acute awareness of the shortcomings of the existing system. It was a time of change, and the women of Prince Edward Island, including myself, began to ask questions of the politicians of the day. There was no doubt about it: childcare was about to become a prominent public issue. Because of the ever-expanding female workforce (both rural and urban), women made it known that more daycare spaces simply must

become available, and improvements in the quality of child care programs for all Island kids must begin to be undertaken. My personal goal
was to help get kids out of cold church basements and daycares set up in
unsafe home recreation rooms. I wanted to see the provincial government
provide capital grants to upgrade salaries and facilities. Quality was an
issue that the community and its early childhood educators took seriously.

The province's Child Care Facilities Board, where I served from 1979
to 1986, inspects and grants licences to child care operators all across the
province. The Early Childhood government staff at that time were Faye
Smith and Kathleen Flanagan. Faye carried out administrative inspections of the facilities, coordinated health and fire inspections, and reported her findings to the Board. She also followed up on recommendations
from the Board should changes need to be made. Kathleen focused on
policy development, provincial funding, and consultations with child care
providers within the sector, along with drafting legislation and regulations.
She was the key person in government who ensured that the granting
program brought in by Premier Ghiz was comprehensive and fair to those
providing care. Over the course of her career, Kathleen would shepherd
in a whole new era of focus on children.

While serving on the Facilities board, I volunteered with the Early
Childhood Development Association on projects and lobbying efforts. It
was in that context that I found myself at a National Child Care Conference in 1981. As part of a panel, I spoke about child care needs from the
family perspective. Many resolutions were passed at the conference, and
an important division occurred: one group would focus on political advocacy and to have the Canadian government establish a national child
care program, while the other group would concentrate on a national strategy for professional development in the child care community. I
chose to support and devote my volunteer time to establishing a national
service-based organization for the child care community that focused on
quality: the Canadian Child Care Federation (CCCF).

My political advocacy began after a Quality of Life Legislative Committee in 1985, where I was lobbying politicians for better quality child
care while parents worked. One Member of the Legislative Assembly

said, "Don't you think parents want too much today? We got along okay with a table and chairs!" Between that comment and others from that in-camera committee hearing, I was shocked to realize there was actually significant political resistance around that table. For most of the men who were MLAs in the legislature at that time, child care, early childhood education, and women working outside the home seemed a foreign concept. I thought naively, that if they only knew and understood, things would change — but as I would come to find out as time passed, it would be another generation before major change took place.

Often publicly, conservative politicians from all political parties would argue that working women would harm the traditional family. The only supportive member at the Quality of Life Committee was Liberal MLA Paul Connolly, who kept nodding his head throughout my presentation and then asked for more details about the recommendations for latch-key kids. One of my suggestions was funding B.L.A.S.T. programs (before, lunch, and after school programs), which could offer programming for children who were going home to an empty house while both parents worked. There were no programs in PEI like this at that time. Because the media was not allowed in the room to hear the presentations or questions, the discussions were not reported and the legislative committee meeting had an air of secrecy to it. The public was in the dark not only about the ideas being proposed, but they were also unaware of the absurd questioning and the old fashioned, chauvinistic attitudes expressed there by some of the Members of the Legislative Assembly. Following my presentation, I was invited to a women's reception hosted by the PEI Advisory Council on the Status of Women in Charlottetown. It was the first "women's reception" that I had ever attended and I was asked by some of the women in attendance about my experience with the secretive legislative committee. The next day, one of the women leaked that conversation to the media. *The Guardian* newspaper happily reported on it a few days later because the secret hearings were a sore point with them, and the meeting soon became infamous. Since my Legislative Committee appearance had been recorded and transcribed, the Chairman, Progressive Conservative MLA Horace Carver, released the whole transcript to *The Guardian* where it was then printed in its entirety. There were two whole pages in the newspaper, exposing the absurdity of the questioning for all to see. I was, however, shocked at the break in confidentiality by the women's reception's leadership. My experience with child care and the negative response from politicians catapulted me in a new direction, and I found myself right in the centre of the PEI women's movement. Soon after, I moved into child care discussions with the PEI Liberal Party, who were in opposition at the time.

From the 1980s onward, the Liberals promised child care improvements on their election platforms, and small changes began to happen incrementally. Coming from the dental community where quality standards and accredited education were important elements, I could understand the enormous need to organize around quality within the child care community.

At the beginning of his government's mandate in 1986, Premier Joseph Ghiz announced much-needed capital grants to improve quality in Island child care centres, with Kathleen Flanagan providing an instrumental advisor role. Thanks to both Premier Joe Ghiz and Kathleen Flanagan, the following year a leading document was released called *Guiding Principles for the Development of Child Care Services*, a groundbreaking initiative for the time. Federally, Liberal governments in Canada discussed child care during election campaigns, made big promises, but did not follow through. The federal Conservatives liked to throw money at parents with tax credits and a do-it-yourself attitude that they called "choice in child care". In fact, only haphazard changes were made for families with working parents in Canada. From a feminist perspective these tax breaks, as generous as they were, did nothing to improve the overall quality in the child care system in the country. Thus, child care centres continued to struggle — as did parents looking for accessible, quality care for their children.

Historically, under the Comprehensive Development Plan of the 1960's many schools across the province consolidated, allowing for private or community-based preschool and kindergarten programs to move into old, ill-equipped community school buildings. Following a comprehensive government review of daycare in 1970, the Department of Social Services became responsible for programming instead of the Department of Education. Under Premier Alex Cambell's government, one early commitment for children happened under the guidance of Honourable Minister Catherine Callbeck. Administered by the Early Childhood Development Association, an early childhood toy lending library was established to ensure children would have access to quality learning materials in their centres, and that these resources were available to all child care directors in both full and part time programs. Circulation of quality learning materials between the centres allowed for better programs and a greater variety for the children.

In the beginning of the organized early childhood years, most of the funding from the government focused on subsidies for "at risk" children, and even then there was a fight to keep pace with facility and staffing costs. The Ghiz grants made improvements to the centres themselves by improving wages, as well as other critical infrastructure. With children's needs and women's challenges in mind, my goal became to help organize toward improving the quality of child care, from my vantage point as a parent. In later years when kindergarten was established, the five year old children moved into the public education system. The government child care offices were then moved back to the education department to form a new department, the Department of Education and Early Childhood Development, reflecting a change from a social service perspective to one of education.

Provisional Executive meeting, Canadian Child Care Federation
L-R: Pam Taylor, Dianne Porter, Sandra Griffin, Front, Karen Chandler

Following the 1981 National Child Care Conference and after subsequent federal government consultation, I became one of five women who volunteered to explore the need for a national organization for the child care community, and the Canadian Child Care Federation (CCCF) was born. We operated as a provisional executive, each of us representing a different region of the country for seven years as we conducted research and laid the groundwork for the new childcare organization.

Sandra Griffin from the Early Childhood program at the University of Victoria, BC represented that province and the North. Sandra acted as the provisional President, chairing the meetings and making local arrangements. Her co-workers at the University of Victoria provided support and encouragement for her efforts. As a single working mother, she knew all too well about the challenges facing parents. And as a former child care educator herself, she held a perspective on quality that was second to none. Following her time as the President of the provisional executive and as a teacher at the University of Victoria, Sandra moved to Ottawa to become the second Executive Director of the Canadian Child Care Federation. When Honourable Ken Dryden was given the mandate by Prime Minister Paul Martin to establish a national child care program, he recruited Sandra as his Chief of Staff.

Karen Chandler represented Ontario, and as an instructor and educator from the Early Childhood Program at George Brown University, she was a tall, glamorous person with a very keen determination to make sure the Ontario perspective was considered. There were many times during her tenure as provisional Vice President where each province would take different positions on issues based on our differing needs. We assured her that Ontario did not have each province's perspective nor all the best practices for all the regions. Thankfully, Karen had a great sense of humour and often pushed ideas to the extreme so we could view the issue in context while her laugh brought all of us the break we sometimes needed. When the Federation hosted its first Annual General Meeting in 1987, Karen became the first President and remained involved for many years as the Federation grew more and more relevant. Today, Karen is writing the seventh edition of a textbook called *Leading for Change: Leadership and Administration of Early Childhood Programs in Canada*, and as of 2022, she is still teaching.

Pamela Taylor, a gentle, warm educator at Grant McEwan Community College in Edmonton, Alberta, represented the western provinces on the provisional executive. The frustrations with the status of child care and the viewpoints she brought to the table were unique to the conservative West. The scope and character of child care in Canada was emerging and Pam's interventions about the political situation in the west kept us open-minded and realistic.

Monique Daviault, the gregarious Québec representative, was a child care provider who shared information about the quickly-evolving child care scene in her province. Her understanding of the needs of Francophone children and their parents was valuable for showcasing child care on the ground in Québec. Her contacts in the Québec early childhood educator's associations kept the two way communication links open and informed. When naming the Federation's first professional magazine, *Interaction*, it was easily understood by both French and English speakers because of her interventions and approval.

As the representative from Atlantic Canada, I was the parent representative and provided the perspectives of Atlantic Canada, when Pam Nadeau could not continue. I had attended the same federal consultation as the other women with Health Canada; so I was very familiar with the goals. Together, we quickly determined the need for more information from those providing care to children, so research became the necessary first step. A national survey was distributed to every program in every province in the country. The main goal of the questionnaire was, "Do you want a national service based organization to support you and your work, and if so, what would be priorities?"

Our small group of five met regularly in Ottawa to create a plan for the future. We flew in from across the country several times a year for three or four days at a time, and camped out in small B&Bs or older, affordable hotels. One such hotel we frequented often was the Lord Elgin, in which we had an old suite where we lived, worked, and held meetings. We also met regularly with Health Canada staff who were supporting our endeavours. Following years of designing, administering our national survey and conducting analysis, our group was ready for the next steps.

We had determined there was high interest and complex needs to develop a quality child care system in the country, and it would need a highly trained and informed workforce. The early childhood community were eager to move forward, with our small group leading the way, towards a formal national organization that would focus on quality care for children. The profession also needed support and services for information sharing among their peers and continued ed-

Canadian Child Care Federation, first Executive Director Diana Smith, Canadian Minister of Health Jake Epp, and provisional President Sandra Griffin

ucation through workshops and conferences. Our aim was to encourage improvements under the banner of quality.

Sandra always brought along a timer and clock to the meetings and kept the discussions focused on the agenda. She was relentless in pushing through an exhausting, lengthy work day to accomplish our current goals, like drafting a constitution and setting new goals for the next marathon meeting that took place usually four months later. There were times in those meetings when we lost track of time trying to get through the agenda, and we worked long days and evenings to get the work done. It was common for us to work through meal times so we had food delivered to the suite. There were often comic salutes to our leader when she pushed too hard, or if the topic of the hour was contentious, we went out for a walk to nearby restaurants in order to get a change of scenery before returning to pick up where we had left off. The cooling off times were necessary when five strong-minded women tried to reach an agreeable consensus on goals and policies as we drafted a new constitution.

In 1985, we applied for funding from Health Canada to hire an Executive Director, and also requested a grant to set up an office in Ottawa. Our first staff person was Diana Smith, an experienced professional who had worked for ten years in a leadership role with the Canadian Home

Economic Association. Her experience at managing a national office and working with a national board of directors would become vital to our future success.

As the provisional Treasurer of the organization I was in constant contact, by courier and phone, with Diana Smith in Ottawa. Today with e-transfers, zoom calls, and email, management would have been much faster. It was not long before we outgrew our small office as we added staff and resources to meet the mandate. We required more funding to further develop the services our research survey had found to be priorities for the profession.

At a tense meeting with Health Canada in our small Parkdale Street office in Ottawa, the provisional executive and Diana answered many questions about our progress and our vision for the future. As Treasurer, I carefully outlined the necessity for our first one million dollar grant in order to move to the next phase of development. Just as I was making my points, Karen relaxed and helped herself to coffee and a muffin which she brought back to the table. As we emphasized our professional development goals, Karen dropped half of the muffin down the front of her blouse. Needless to say, it was a much-needed icebreaker and took our tense meeting from funds provider and client to the beginning of a friendly relationship between CCCF and Health Canada that has prevailed over many years, remaining strong due to good communication and a few laughs along the way.

I served for many years, representing Atlantic Canada, until the first annual meeting when individual provinces and territories elected Board representatives and adopted the constitution. This first AGM was held in Winnipeg in 1987, following the CCCF's first conference. It was important to many of us that the Federation's first conference be held in Winnipeg, the location of that first child care conference in 1981 so many years before where the idea of creating a national association of early childhood educators was conceived. More than fifteen hundred delegates had created the idea of a professional-based association, and we had developed and grown as a fledgling organization with hundreds of country-wide participants and members in strong support. The CCCF had

Celebrating the opening of the first office of the Canadian
Child Care Federation, Ottawa
L-R: Sandra, Dianne, Monique, Pam and Karen

met that goal and it was time for me to move on to other challenging public issues relating to women and children.

Cathy MacCormack was elected by the Early Childhood Education Association of PEI to be the Island's first Board member going forward. The other Atlantic provinces also elected their members and at the AGM a truly representative Board emerged. At the same meeting, an elected National Executive was formed to lead the initiative into the future.

At federal and provincial meetings and conferences, the trends around child care were easy to map over time. A scan demonstrated that the Canadian women's movement and the child care profession were on the same page when it came to creating services for children, but there were deep divisions, one of which was the creation of the Canadian Child Care Advocacy Association (CCCAA), funded by Status of Women Canada. Concerned with the slow pace of change, political lobbying for publicly funded, non-profit child care began in earnest. However, both national organizations had one goal in common: the Federation and CCCAA both worked to improve the quality of care for the nation's children.

In the 1980s and 1990s there was a global shift towards neo-liberal thought, and in PEI the government was under pressure from the bond rating agencies to pay the debt off, reduce the deficit, and follow the developing global plan. The PEI priorities were set by the government of the day and the changes within the PEI Public Service were then implemented. Reforms of government were coordinated by the Office of Government Reform on PEI. The thinking at the time, both within government and amongst its senior management, was to cultivate a belief that government should promote individual responsibility, with an emphasis on the individual for generating life chances. The idea was also to create a smaller, leaner civil service.

Child care was an important provincial concern for Premier Joseph Ghiz, however he was preoccupied with the biggest financial challenge of his government. Provincially, when he was first elected he introduced direct grants to qualifying child care centres and was fortunate to have Kathleen Flanagan as an experienced, well educated advisor. Her work has been a key factor in the successes we have had here in PEI for more than forty years.

UNSUNG HERO
CATHY MacCORMACK

If there was one person who epitomized excellence in her profession with children, it was Cathy MacCormack. She was instrumental in working with others in her profession on projects and lobbying for the benefit of children. As the national representative, keeping the PEI Early Childhood Development Association informed and involved in the Canadian Child Care Federation was her constant priority, and she served for many

years as the Island's representative. Two of her most challenging and rewarding accomplishments were serving as Co-Chairperson of both the 1987 Winnipeg Child Care conference and the 1990 Charlottetown CCCF conference called, 'Children: The Heart of the Matter'.

Throughout her career, Cathy was instrumental in bringing community and government together; she was a true collaborator. She was a public servant from 1987-2015, and in 2014 she won the Lieutenant Governor's Award for Excellence in Public Administration. Her career began on the front lines as an early childhood educator in the early 1980's, with her later taking on a position of Early Childhood Resource with the PEI government in 1987. Her entire career focused on the well-being of children.

As a young mother, Cathy was always directly involved as team coach or manager for many of the sports and other activities her children were involved with. Her daughter, Denine Hancock, describes an involved, caring, and committed mother who never failed to show up at sporting events, and if team leadership was needed she stepped in to help out. If there was something her children were doing, Cathy was supportive and encouraging. If her children were involved, then so was Cathy.

Within the Early Childhood Development Association of PEI Cathy was a team player and leader, serving as its Secretary-Treasurer for eight years before becoming a civil servant in 1987. Cathy stayed on as the PEI representative to the Canadian Child Care Federation as part of her professional development, where she demonstrated her leadership skills while bringing the PEI perspective to the table. Cathy passed away in April, 2015.

CATHY MacCORMACK
UNSUNG HERO

UNSUNG HERO
KATHLEEN FLANAGAN

The summer of 1975 was a beautiful time of year on the Island; a time when many 20-somethings "from away" were discovering PEI for the first time. I fell in love with PEI on my first visit — love at first sight! With a background in early childhood education, I quickly met some Island women who invited me to a meeting of the newly formed Early Childhood Development Association of PEI. Along with many others, I stayed. By January 1976, I established the first Montessori centre in PEI at Poole's Corner, operating in the newly-built Tourist Information Centre during the off season. Forty six years later, the Montessori Children's Centre still operates as an Early Years Centre in Montague, with hundreds if not thousands of children having attended.

My growing interest in research and policies affecting early childhood education and the educators who teach young children led me to take employment as "Coordinator of Early Childhood Services" for the PEI government at a time when the idea of an early childhood sector on PEI was just emerging. Although various forms of government funding for early childhood services had been in place since the early 1970s (when the Development Plan provided free child care in selected centres across PEI), by the late 70s that very targeted approach was changed to allow eligible families across PEI access to funding to help with the cost. But it wasn't enough — and by the mid-1980s Premier Joe Ghiz introduced the first PEI direct funding program for licensed centres, providing funds for wages and to improve program quality. It wasn't just about the money — it was a recognition that early childhood education mattered, and that it had benefits for children, families, and society. The funding recognized that the people who taught young children mattered, and that the government valued the quality of these programs for young children. It was an exciting day for the early childhood sector in PEI, and I still have Premier Ghiz's hand-written note of thanks to me for the work involved in making it happen.

While progress in policy development often seemed slow, it was steady. In the following years, early years experiences came to be appreciated as key indicators of health, well-being, success in school and in life events, and even influencing the next generation. National initiatives brought greater profile and resources to the sector.

As the saying goes, "it's a small world," and by the turn of the century my interest in early childhood policy on an international level was strong. I decided to leave government and venture out on my own, working as a consultant here in Canada and around the world. My four young children weren't so young anymore, and my new work commitments took me to Asia, Africa, and the Middle East — many times with my husband joining me for additional travel and adventure. International work is fascinating, with the challenge it presents to take what you know and re-examine that knowledge in the context of another culture, and often another political reality.

Although I've worked around the world and for just about every province and territory, my heart is in PEI. I've done research and strategic policy development for different Island governments, resulting in a re-designed early childhood system, an early learning curriculum framework, a workforce strategy, and updated recommendations on future early learning policy development for the Island. I'm grateful to see that my little grandchildren are benefitting from this work!

But the real credit goes to PEI's early childhood educators. They are professional, hard-working, and committed. They take new policy directions and curriculum guidance and make it come alive for children and families — and that is what really matters.

KATHLEEN FLANAGAN
UNSUNG HERO

Many inconsistencies exist in the varied quality of children's services that are accessible while parents work, and the reasons that some great places become inaccessible when parents are searching for care are even more varied still. The fees can be too high for some families, and even if the family may qualify for a care subsidy, often there are still not enough child care spaces available. Waiting lists for subsidies grew longer as more and more women entered the full time workforce.

In 2006, when I visited my grandchildren at their centres in Ottawa while both parents worked, I was always impressed by the caring staff who worked with the children. To me, qualified caring staff is, and continues to be, the most important factor in choosing quality care. Among early childhood educators, staff turnover was always a concern as they moved on to better paying jobs in the better funded, more expensive facilities. Some left the profession altogether for work where their pay was better than in the child care system. The profession lost many qualified, competent people over the years due to low wages.

My grandchildren are no longer using child care services. In 2021, the announcement of a National Child Care Program by Prime Minister Justin Trudeau promised to change the quality of care and the salary levels in child care centres for early childhood educators across the country. The intentions are good and will mean more affordable, better quality care for children and will provide necessary support for women and their families. Perhaps my great grandchildren will be its beneficiaries.

I continue to be concerned for children and have spent some of my volunteer time since 2005 working as a member of the Board of Directors for a local camp for high risk children, The Appin Road Children's Camp. At a presentation to the charitable organization "100 Women Who Care", Camp Director Ruth Lacey made the case for donating to the camp by providing some history of the camp, its mission and goals. I have a great deal of respect for Ruth, who has committed forty years of leadership and direct involvement day-to-day as the camp director.

This was part of her presentation:

UNSUNG HERO
RUTH LACEY

As adults, if you and I need to work on a problem, we can sit down and talk about it. A child doesn't learn and change that way; it happens through living and playing. I can remember the moment I looked at a child across the table where he sat in my Charlottetown office and I thought, "This is not the way to help him," and in that moment in 1980, "Camp" was born.

The Appin Road Children's Camp mission is to serve at-risk troubled children and youth and their families. It is a living group therapy — mainly through their attending an 8 week summer day camp program that is recreational, educational, and therapeutic.

The Camp takes 15 different children each summer. Who are these children? Most but not all come from low socioeconomic, dysfunctional families where they often experience neglect or abuse and violence of various forms. Many face extreme adversities in their lives that can influence their behaviour and ability to learn. They may exhibit school refusal, high anxiety, violence, self-harm, low self-esteem, and low self-regulation.

The Camp is located in the country and at the shore. Nature in itself is healing and there is lots of free playtime to swim, look for sea glass, use the paddle board and kayak. They curl up with books and play with puzzles, Lego, the train set, or the zip-line.

One summer, it was popular to build forts with sheets, tarpaulins, clothes pins and tree branches. At Camp there is lots of music, poetry, and exposure to the arts. At Camp they experience a sense of belonging, wonder, and joy.

There are many structured requirements: baking, sewing, carpentry, and musical instruments. They can learn to play a trumpet or experience violin lessons. The most popular excursion is a day with Yogi Fell at her

As a former member of the camp Board of Directors, our main role is fundraising and governance issues. We worked to keep the camp totally self-sufficient with no government money for its operations. The annual fundraising drive each winter collects the funds to pay tuition to supplement parents' fees. Many parents cannot afford to pay full fees so the fundraising is critical for the children.

For many years the campers would visit my cottage as one of many field trips, to take part in spiritual activities around the labyrinth on the property. It always amazed me that the kids "got it". Their path was not easy, not a straight line and sometimes with rough corners to move around. When walking the path of the labyrinth they are reminded of camp lessons: to trust their path, that they are not alone, that they must accommodate other children who are on the path, and that they must take the time to reflect and slow down, especially when times are tough.

The Gifted

They come along often — the gifted.
These youth, in moments of their lightness
Where the pain of past ignorance
Gives way to hope and love.

The sadness and distress — of the poor,
Of the children
Breaks our soul and makes reality
Hard to bear.

Youth is a time of clear, pure hope
Where we can not only watch
Their transformation
From egg to sage

But, they are what we are waiting for
To show us their new vision.
As we marvel at seeing the best of the future,
We climb up off our knees.

The youth of our country can heal our brokenness.
They can resurrect our spirit
With their innocence.
They are the miracle of our future.

—Dianne Porter, January 2022

Chapter Four:
Through the Gender Lens

For many years, I have been asked about what constitutes a "women's issue" and I say, "It is like learning to see in the dark." Women's experiences have seldom been a focus in the formal public education system; in the history books, we were invisible. Bringing information about women and girls forward sheds light in the darkness, and once you can see in the dark, the issues begin to emerge. The viewpoint of women is critical, the gendered lens which focuses on the female experience both acute and essential. I believe it is vital for governments to govern with two eyes open, with both men and women working together to grasp a fuller picture of a situation or circumstance. The lives of girls and women must be considered when making decisions, and are certainly just as important as the experiences of boys and men.

In 1988, I was invited to speak at the Hillsborough Rotary Club, when the membership was considering whether to change their policy to include women members. In trying to keep things light, I opened with a comment that walking in there was, "like walking into a room of dinosaurs." Most of the men laughed, as was my intention. Some did not. My speech gave an overview of the work we were doing at the PEI Advisory Council on the Status of Women, and the need for gender-based analysis of issues and situations. By utilizing women's knowledge and ideas, one would be better able to consider all points of view and avoid the common mistake of a narrow-minded policy. I argued that to be inclusive, we all need to see the world with two eyes open, which in turn would provide a new depth of perception. The group thanked me for coming, and said they were indeed interested in broadening their horizons. The media were present at that meeting; however, reported only that, "Porter calls the Rotary Club Dinosaurs." Through my years of lobbying for change that would improve the status of women, there were dozens of encounters with the media who put their own spin on what was said — I would just have to grow a thicker skin and develop a media strategy.

To study public policies and make recommendations, it is vital that there be a direct relationship between what we know and what we do. A robust data set about the inclusion of women needs to be examined closely, and problems arise when there is insufficient or unreliable information. In terms better understood by today's standards, one might say that evidence-based research about the experiences of girls and women is necessary, and so is access to critical segregated data.

At the United Nations Fourth Conference on Women in 1995, Canada formally adopted a policy of Gender Based Analysis (GBA); a policy that was to be applied across government and inform the policy decision making process so that errors and omissions would not be made when formulating policy, programs, and services. What I see as most important, and indeed essential, is that policies be the product of democratic deliberation, facilitated by government policy analysts who conduct GBA. At that time, Canada ratified this policy and Status of Women Canada undertook a training program for policy analysts within the federal public service. It was a step ahead.

With this new community-based research about women and girls during the second wave of feminism in the 1970s and 1980s, there came a wave of interest in Island history and a call for public advocacy to change the status quo. Women all across the country mobilized to lobby for change in their own communities, now supported by federal assistance for community development. Following the creation of the Canadian Charter of Rights and Freedoms, PEI women were now part of a movement. The gender-based analysis that began in the community soon progressed to the level of government policy analysts.

Targeted federal funds were allocated to the province of PEI, and both the Women's Network and the East Prince Women's Information Centre (EPWIC) received funds. Soon, small projects began with the process of networking and providing information about women's equality, in the context of the Charter. Through the Women's Network, the Island's first magazine by, for, and about Island women was produced called *Common Ground*. Anne McCallum was the Editor, Writer, and Photographer for the magazine. Another important facet of the Women's Network were the rural workshops. Dianne Hicks Morrow was hired to coordinate with local rural women to determine which topics they might like to hear more about, and during these workshops local issues were presented by bringing in guest speakers. For many years Dianne Hicks Morrow also coordinated the annual Women's Festival, a two day event full of workshops, guest speakers, music and silent auctions for fundraising, and good times. As Board members at the Network for a short time, we were better able to gear funding for projects to meet the needs of women.

In Summerside, The East Prince Women's Information Centre (EPWIC) was opened to provide education and support to the women's community, and there was a good network of women providing ongoing qualitative research on issues as they arose, which they shared with the community, researchers, and governments. Both Women's Network and EPWIC have been in operation for more than four decades.

UNSUNG HERO
DIANNE HICKS MORROW

As the mother of two young sons living in an all-male home, my feminist instincts had to flower or wilt. Reading *Common Ground* magazine was one way to nurture those instincts, and I still recall being upset that horrible road conditions kept me from attending the first Women's Festival. Little did I know when I read about it in the next issue of *Common Ground* that I'd end up as coordinator of the following festival a year later, as part of my new job as Women's Network's project coordinator. To settle me into this newly-created half-time position in the WN office, its only other employee, the editor of *Common Ground* Anne McCallum, guided me into writing interviews and articles for the magazine, which was a wonderful way for me to learn more about the organization. While there had been one festival already, with a strong volunteer committee, my other main project was a first for Women's Network: to organize three rural seminars for women across the Island, one each in East and West Prince and the third in Kings County. I recall the panic I felt about making cold calls to strangers to invite them to be a local volunteer planning committee. Wise community developer Bea Mair gave me the best advice: if you want to reach the whole county, choose a location that all communities use already. For example, since Bea lived in Georgetown, her advice was to hold the Kings County seminar at Poole's Corner, where people were used to going for wedding receptions, political rallies, dances, and dinners, rather than in either Souris or Montague. In West Prince she suggested Westisle School, where all high school students went, not O'Leary or Alberton or Tignish. The risk of holding a seminar in one particular community was that only its own women would attend. Bea was right, with the Westisle seminars routinely attracting around a hundred women of all ages. Her other sage advice was to include a woman of each political stripe on each planning committee. Of course, I had no clue, but she promptly gave me a selection of Liberal, Conservative, and NDP names to contact. Thus, the event could not be labelled with any one political stripe, and it was guaranteed excellent promotion by all parties. Seminar topics ranged from mothering to environmental issues and political lobbying. The generosity of all those excellent volunteers, from farm women to fishers, stay-at-home moms to minimum wage workers, taught me much about community development. Each year, I'd worry as I reached out to the volunteers that maybe they were tired of hearing from me. But, without fail, they'd invite even more women to join their committees and the seminar attendance continued to grow. To this day, it's exciting when I run into any of those women from across the Island. One of my main concerns was that Women's Network should not be seen as some fringe organization of flaky feminists — I began my ten years there in 1985, don't forget. While a few of the WN

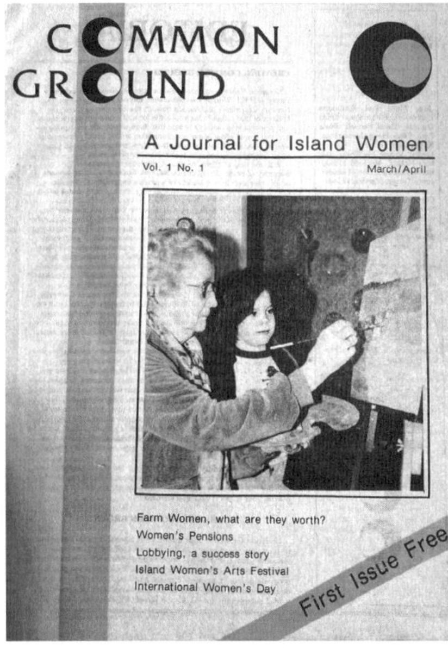

Cover of the first edition of COMMON GROUND,
a magazine for and about Island Women

volunteer Board members felt I should introduce myself as a feminist, I balked at the use of labels of any kind. In my life I'd navigated having a blind mother and my own polio damage without talking or writing about either until my mid-forties. I felt labels created immediate barriers; that it was better to interact woman-to-woman with my volunteer committees, letting our beliefs emerge naturally. For me, it was a dream come true to see a Women's Festival, workshops run by the Women's Institute, and even one facilitated by the Lesbian Collective. The over two hundred women at that festival bonded and learned from each other all weekend. Similarly, I was gratified by the reaction of rural seminar planning committees when I passed out festival brochures that used not only the 'f' word (feminist) but also the 'l' word (lesbian). One very quiet, shy woman spoke up to say how pleased she was that Women's Network was bringing this into the open, and how much it would help her sister, who lived in fear.

Logo and theme for the PEI Women's Festival in 1987. Silk screening on linen towel.
There were also festival t-shirts for sale by Doreen and Chum.

Speaking of fear, several rural seminar women with clout in their communities and who worked on provincial organizations told me they supported the right of a woman to control their pregnancies, but they were afraid to speak up in public. For over thirty years, Women's Network and other organizations had lobbied for a women's right to choose. On April 1, 2016, Premier Wade MacLauchlan said that his government's decision to provide abortion services on PEI, "was made now because of the time frame set by a pending legal challenge that sought to force the province to provide full and unrestricted access to publicly funded abortion services on the Island."

I worked at the Women's Network for ten challenging and exhilarating years — the longest I've stayed at any job. Besides making lifelong friendships, working there was more educational than taking another university degree — political studies and community development in action. I left Women's Network to switch roles from advocacy to literacy. Next I became a member of the LM Montgomery Institute for two years before retiring when my husband did, to enable us to travel while physically able. The writing skills fostered by Women's Network and Literacy Alliance led me to take some creative writing courses at UPEI. I won various awards and eventually had two books of poetry and two non-fiction books published by Acorn Press. In 2008 the Award for Contribution to the Literary Arts was given to me, in part for my years teaching Writing from Life at PEI Seniors College. In 2012 my second poetry book won the PEI Book Award and in 2013 I was named PEI Poet Laureate for three years. Grandchildren entered my life in 2013 and now I help them write their own books.

DIANNE HICKS MORROW
UNSUNG HERO

UNSUNG HERO
ANDY LOU SOMERS

For the past 25 years, I have worked at the East Prince Women's Information Centre (EPWIC), where I am the Executive Director. As a mother of six children it has been a passion of mine to be a good role model and a positive support to them. I am committed to improving women's lives: I am passionate about women's equality, I help women navigate through government programs which can help them, and I lobby governments. I also provide an eight-week Women's Employability Program since 2012, and I love the work that I do.

As a woman of the 1960's who turns seventy this year, I have always had a sense of fairness and justice. I remember having a 'sit-in' at the Summerside high school to allow girls to wear pants to school. We were wearing mini skirts anyway, and it seemed absurd that pants were the concern of the school board, when some of those skirts were pretty short.

Before I came on staff, the Founders of EPWIC included Molly Bell and Isabelle Christian as board members and the first Executive Director was Doris MacDonald. The Coordinator was Angie Cormier from Abrams Village.

There are many different avenues to the work of EPWIC. We have lobbied for many years for the Women's Wellness Centre for the Prince County Hospital and we are pleased that reproductive health is part of that service. In the Women's Program for Employability, the women come for a twelve week comprehensive program introducing them to work in the community and improving their ability to successfully find employment. Sometimes skills need to be strengthened, so during four of the weeks the students work 'on the job' in areas where they hope to find work in the future. We have an 80% success rate of helping them find connections to future work.

Every year on December 6th, we host a memorial service for the young women engineering students who were killed in the Montreal Massacre. At the same time, we honour and remember those Island women lost to intimate partner violence. We have been able to work with the community and the city of Summerside to create a permanent memorial at Heather Moyce Park on Ottawa Street.

Currently we are applying for charitable status so we might do fundraising instead of just relying on government grants. Without core funding, our work is limited to government priorities. I was thrilled to learn from the City of Summerside that I would be receiving the Queen's Jubilee Medal for the work I have done with EPWIC, in partnership with the city and other community groups. One of our most successful lobbying campaigns was to reinstate family legal aid in the province. We partnered with Women's Network to advocate for almost four years to get it done. One thing I have learned in this job for sure —is how to lobby the government for change.

ANDY LOU SOMERS
UNSUNG HERO

UNSUNG HERO
ANNE McCALLUM

Writing about myself doesn't come to me easily. I'm far happier highlighting other people's stories, which is what I've done for much of my life in Canada. I moved to Ottawa from Dumfries, Scotland in 1973, with high hopes and a newly-conferred MA in English from the University of Aberdeen. Eventually, Carleton University offered me a position — as a daycare worker. Not at all the exciting career I'd hoped to start in my new country, but my best option as an immigrant and a woman at the time. While I came to realize that the loving attention we gave the children in our care was invaluable, I could see that Canadian society held the opposite view. The wage was minimal; the status was low. All my co-workers, of course, were women.

When I relocated to rural PEI with my husband in 1977, I'd spent the previous year as a news and features writer at the *Aylmer Reporter* near Gatineau. By then we'd become keen environmentalists and members of the burgeoning back-to-land movement. As we established our family in PEI and gradually set ourselves up as organic farmers, I naturally gravitated towards writing about agriculture. I developed a huge respect for the commitment and resilience of local food producers through countless interviews on farms from Tignish to Souris. My stories were published in *Farm Focus, Rural Delivery,* and *The Island Farmer.*

The public image of a farmer was, at that time, exclusively male. It became obvious to me that women's contributions to their family farms were at least equal to men's, and sometimes greater. Women managed the accounts, held off-farm jobs, fed workers, raised children, tended animals, and harvested crops. And they participated in rural women's groups as well. The word "multitasking" didn't even come close to describing it. A new organization called Women in Support of Agriculture invited me to tell that important story through audio-visual presentations featuring eight of their members. I think that's when I first understood the value of feminism.

In September 1981, I responded to an ad from the recently-established PEI Women's Network Project Committee for a part-time editor of a new women's publication, as yet undeveloped. To my great joy, they chose me to pull together the first issue to be published in March 1982. I ended up serving as editor of PEI's first feminist magazine for thirteen unforgettable years. *Common Ground*, as we named it, helped build a sense of shared purpose in the women's community long before the invention of the Internet. It acted as a forum for women's groups determined to change our institutions, laws, and behaviours so that we would enjoy the same political, social, and economic rights as men. We reported on the national and international feminist movements of the 80s and 90s. We created a supportive place for women to express their ideas in poetry and prose. We told stories about those of us who were knocking down the gender barrier to build careers in non-traditional areas. We also profiled women who were making important contributions to their communities in a multitude of ways across the Island, as movers and shakers in politics, health, education, agriculture, fishing, and everything else. Those were the stories that I loved to tell. From day one, being the *Common Ground* editor was always considerably more than a paid job for me. It was a true labour of love.

As my kids became old enough, they helped me with the mail-out, affixing labels, checking postal codes, and inserting subscription flyers. Like all not-for-profit roles, it was demanding and dependent on unpaid contributions from staff and volunteers alike. But for the first time, I felt committed to something larger than my own life and family.

The proud, determined, diverse women who helped create and develop our magazine became my friends and my community. Of course it wasn't all golden. Some Islanders were offended when we discussed hot-button issues like abortion, different sexual orientations, or even wage equality. I remember a female clerk in a Charlottetown magazine store telling me she'd like to "throw that rag on the back of the fire" when I asked her to distribute the magazine for us. But she was part of a small minority. We persisted in working for change using the magazine as our forum year after year and I believe we ultimately made a positive difference in women's lives on PEI. When I left the editor's role after thirteen remarkable years with Women's Network, it was with great sadness. But I moved on to a new challenge as Regional Coordinator of the Atlantic Breast Cancer Partnership, supported by Health Canada.

This was still the pre-internet era and there was a huge need for up-to-date information resources about breast cancer treatments and supports to empower newly-diagnosed women and their families. The partnership we created to help meet that demand involved four divisions of the Canadian Cancer Society, numerous national, regional, and provincial health organizations, oncology professionals, and of course breast cancer survivors themselves. We developed newsletters, information kits, resource guides, and support group lists, and we ran a 1-800 information/support line. It was a major challenge to coordinate this unwieldy partnership.

As always, the satisfaction came from the incredible commitment of the organization's volunteers — and from hearing and telling the women's personal stories about how they faced great adversity and, in many cases at least, managed to overcome it by supporting each other.

When I first met Claire Arsenault, she worked with the federal government's Women's Program and reviewed applications for funding from community groups seeking funds to advance the status of women. I was part of a small group who would consult with Claire at Off Broadway, a small Charlottetown restaurant, to discuss projects and strategies about how to strengthen grant applications. Without Claire, these early feminist organizations would not have been successful and some initiatives would not even have happened. Feminists owe her a debt of gratitude, as do other BIPOC groups she subsequently assisted in later years. She negotiated on behalf of Island women, and they thrived because of her behind the scenes management skills.

It was apparent to many in the community that violence against women was a major issue that was well hidden and seldom discussed. When a small group of advocates for change decided to explore creating a shelter for abused women and their children, it became an uphill battle. The construction and establishment of Anderson House was something that caused debate in the community. Calls came in from those who chastised the group for "breaking up families." The small, determined core collective group, led by Julie Devon Dodd, worked with the staff at Canada Mortgage and Housing to fund the project, including locating a property, and bringing the building up to CMHC national standards as well as fire building codes for PEI.

Ann Sherman from the Voluntary Resource Council staff organized meeting space and sat in as part of the planning group. Jill Lightwood became part of the collective who worked with women and children at the house for many years and very soon after opening, Jan Devine joined the staff when she was only twenty-four years old. Today, forty years later, Jan just retired from her work at Anderson House with traumatized women and children who suffer abuse.

UNSUNG HERO
CLAIRE ARSENAULT

On my thirty-first birthday in 1980, I started a job at the Secretary of State Department. I had finished two years of international development projects in Southeast Asia, and had been back home in PEI for about a year after. Little did I realize what an extraordinary opportunity for meaningful work this new job would present to me, and the timing couldn't have been better.

During the early 80s, women's groups were organizing around specific issues demanding to be heard and understood. The Secretary of State Department could provide financial assistance and development support to help increase their effectiveness in bringing about social change. The Charlottetown office of the department had two social development officers ready to work with the community. Our main programs focused on minority official language groups: First Nations, Multiculturalism, women, people with disabilities, human rights education, and voluntary action.

The Women's Program was the only funding program specifically designed to improve the status of women on the Island, and I soon met with many groups and committees already organized around equality issues in order to promote the program, support the work of existing groups, and assist newer groups to become program eligible. In PEI, we had women in agriculture and fishing, First Nations women, newcomer/immigrant women: Les Femmes Acadienne, Women's Institutes, Transition House Association, and East Prince Women were all organizations doing work in these areas. There was also a number of ad hoc committees of women organized around equality issues related to the labour force and economy, violence against women, women in the arts, health issues and legal rights.

The energy was amazing.

These groups of volunteers were donating time and skills to work towards improving the lives of women. Even with very limited financial assistance, the advancement in public understanding of the gender-based issues facing women and the need for social change was undeniable. Following a province-wide research and consultation process with women active in their communities, it was agreed that there was a need for inter-group communication and collaboration. This gave birth to *Common Ground* and the Women's Network Inc., which both became valuable assets in advancing equality issues for women.

For me, in the midst of all this activity and as a development professional, I felt immense respect and solidarity for the work undertaken by all these small groups of committed women who made big accomplishments. This early work laid the foundation for institutional change at the provincial level and many of these organizations still exist almost forty years later, supporting and serving women in PEI. Bravo!

The Multicultural Program was also a significant game changer in raising awareness of equality issues affecting newcomers and people of colour on PEI. Providing financial and organizational support to the minority cultural community gave visibility to issues that needed public recognition. Racism, cross-cultural understanding, integration and retention, and systemic bias in our structures were some of the major issues that needed to be addressed. Over the years, the work from the 1980s and 90s, together with changes in government policies and pressures, morphed into further consolidation within the PEI Association for Newcomers. The founding members of this organization also have a lot to be proud of, and deserve our recognition.

Working with the Mi'kmaq and other Indigenous peoples of PEI was another area of responsibility. In my position, I spent lots of time with a number of prominent community leaders, elders, and individuals involved in improving the lives of their members. What a transformative opportunity it was for me to be able to develop a more complete understanding of First Nations' issues, history, challenges, cultural celebrations, arts and medicines, and dogged perseverance. It serves me to this day.

Since retirement in 2010, I have shoestring travelled far and wide; I have grown into an artisan creating wonderful window jewellery with crystal prisms, I have seen my son and daughter launch their lives, I have two grandchildren who stole my heart, I do exercise classes to keep me active and make me happy, and I have a partner and two dogs who help fill my life. I still have brothers and sisters whom I see as often as I can as well as dear friendships that nurture me both here and away. Trust me, it was not all sunshine and roses but I am very grateful to have made my small mark on the world.

CLAIRE ARSENAULT
UNSUNG HERO

UNSUNG HERO
JAN DEVINE

When I arrived in PEI in 1982, I was twenty-four years old. I had travelled across the country in my 1967 Volkswagen camper van, and when I got to PEI, I stayed. Here I have many life-long friends, many of whom I met in the Island Peace Walk, which took place just months after we arrived.

I began my career at Anderson House as a volunteer, working with the children when their moms needed time to plan. I was hired in August of 1983, and have worked there ever since. Although the pay was low, I loved the work. In later years I helped unionize our staff and have been the shop steward ever since that time. The pay and benefits

Jan and Lee Fleming, part of the founding group of organizers, attend the first PEI Gay Pride Parade.

have slowly crept upward and I am proud of having helped to make that happen.

Over the past thirty nine years, we have accomplished a lot with the families who used our services, and I believe we did so with a wonderful staff. Although it is not a tangible item that is easy to quantify, we moved consciousness forward on family violence in the province by bringing the "unseen" to light.

In my early years I was a social activist: women and militarism, Women's Festival, Women's Network, PEI Advisory Council on the Status of Women, setting up the first gay/lesbian support line, becoming a member of the Coalition Against Pornography, and organizing dozens of women's dances and events. I was also part of a group in the 1980s and 90s who made it our purpose to make the gay and lesbian community more visible.

With an interest in music, I travelled to the Michigan Women's music festival for six summers and worked on the day stage and as a carpenter. There I was able to meet many excellent performers, some who I was able to bring to PEI for the Women's Festival to serve as keynote speakers or performers, which greatly enriched our local festival.

In my later years, I worked with US singer-songwriter Carolyn McDade and co-produced four projects which created CDs of choral singing music. These highlighted women singing love songs to the earth — and taking care of all our deep connections in life using the power of the human voice speaking truth to make change in our societies and our lives. These projects involved women from PEI, Atlantic Canada, as well as other parts of the country and the United States.

Now, in 2022 at the age of sixty-five, I am getting ready to retire from Anderson House. I will try to remain hopeful on the continuance of the work that makes lives more peaceful for women and children. Some days I succeeded better than others, but every day I tried.

UNSUNG HERO
ANN SHERMAN

In September of 1979, I moved to PEI and luckily rented a house around the corner from Ellie Reddin. I volunteered at the Voluntary Resource Council and soon was offered a contract position where I met leaders of many volunteer organizations from across the Island. By 1981 I was volunteering with Ellie and another woman, Kirsten Martin, where I  started the Island Peace Committee to lobby against the testing of cruise missiles in Canada. I travelled to New York with the NS Voice of Women for the Second Special Session on Disarmament at the United Nations.

By 1985, I had gone to work for the Community Legal Information Association, where I stayed until 2012. I became the Executive Director in 1989, and enjoyed my career with CLIA until my retirement after twenty seven years of working on important legal and social justice issues.

Since I was heavily into crime prevention through social justice, I was appointed to the National Crime Prevention Council — an extraordinary three years that enabled me to meet Canadians from Nain, Newfoundland to Victoria, British Columbia. From 2004-2009 I served as a Commissioner for the PEI Human Rights Commission. Over the years I was active in many organizations that explored women's issues, peace, and social justice. I made presentations to many government committees, both federal and provincial, and I lobbied for the change that I felt was needed.

As an active volunteer in the community I served on many boards and associations which both reflect my priorities but also my mission in life:

Family Violence Prevention Services
Judicial Advisory Committees AIDSPEI/PEERS Alliance
Premier's Action Committee on Family Violence Prevention
Victims of Crime Advisory Committees Task Force on Access to
Justice
Canadian Paraplegic Association
Quality of Island Life Cooperative
Rotary Club of Charlottetown Royalty
National Association of Women and the Law

ANN SHERMAN
UNSUNG HERO

Thirty years after Anderson House opened, I was involved as a fund-raiser to remodel and refurbish the house. Senator Catherine Callbeck and I had toured the facility and had spoken to house staff about the conditions after high use over so many years. Following the tour, it was decided that a committee was needed to raise the funds to do the repairs and renovations that would better serve the clients and their children.

I set up a meeting with the Executive Director of Family Violence Prevention Services, Phil Matusiewicz, to discuss establishing a community committee to plan the project and raise the funds. Carolyn Bertram, who was Community and Cultural Affairs Minister at the time, committed a community improvement grant of $100,000 to do some of the work. The civil servants in the department kept telling us that we were not qualified to receive the grants aimed at community improvement. To me, there was no better example of community than fundraising for a critical shelter for abused women and children. Our persistence paid off and the grant money arrived. Phil was then able to work with staff and contractors to develop the renovation plans and timelines. The total budget for the completed renovation became a $300,000 project.

MLA Valerie Docherty agreed to chair the community fundraising committee and almost single-handedly was able to secure in-kind

Phil and Valerie in the new kitchen at
Anderson House

donations from local businesses for many materials and supplies. Valerie believed that the kitchen had become the heart of the house, and placed a high priority on having a new and well-equipped kitchen. Home Hardware willingly supplied the kitchen cupboards at a greatly reduced price, Birt's Furniture supplied the kitchen appliances, Paderno donated all the supplies such as pots and pans, dishes and baking utensils, saying, "Just come to the store and choose what you need."

The Brick donated the large dining room table and chairs, and the industrial grade food preparation island was manufactured and donated by Island Fabricators. My requests to Leon's furnished the living room with sturdy leather furniture, tables, and a new television, and Hambly's provided bedroom furniture. Valerie refurbished a bedroom as her own personal donation, covering the bed with a quilt she had made by hand. A local decorator, Stephanie Mowy donated her skills and time to select and coordinate materials, colour schemes for the flooring, wall paints, and window coverings. Peter and I sponsored the refurbishment of the children's play space with the assistance of Owl's Hollow, creating a fun new place for children in stressful times. The third floor was renovated and new stairways were added since the offices of Family Violence Prevention Services were going to be relocated from formerly rented space in the city. It was a wonderful example of a community coming together to get the job done.

The house reconstruction was very well coordinated by Phil Matusiewicz, who was able to work with contractors and tradespeople. One very interesting connection he made was with Women's Network's program called Trade HERizons, coordinated by Sara Roach Lewis. The women training in traditional male trades were learning on the job and performed skilled trades work throughout the reconstruction of the house. I remember watching them apply the seam filling on the newly repaired, and newly built walls.

UNSUNG HERO
SARA ROACH LEWIS

When I was a young girl in the eighties, I attended the women's festivals hosted by Women's Network. It took me a long time to understand why these weekends had such a profound impact and ultimately shaped my career and my life. Growing up as a girl in rural PEI, there was not always interest or space for my voice to talk about what was important to me, but at those festivals there was.

I always believed our role at Women's Network was to create a safe and welcoming space, and to invite women (and girls) to bring the magic: the magic that comes from shared experiences, a desire for equity and equality, and the drive to improve the community for all. Women's Network was a place where you planted seeds. Some germinated quickly, and others took years, but the result was a perpetual garden full of beautiful flowers, plants, and trees.

I like to say that I wore all the hats at Women's Network. I was recruited to join the board in my late 20s for my youthful voice. Given that I turned fifty in 2022, that was not yesterday! I was Board Chair from 2005-2007 and supported the management through a challenging time for the organization. When my youngest was eleven months old, I joined the organization as a part-time Project Coordinator, then I transitioned to Project Manager and eventually I became the Executive Director, a role that I held for almost four years. In 2016, I became a mentor to the incoming Executive Director Jillian Killfoil and provided consulting support for the team for several years. I am proud of our collaborative approach to guiding the organization through a critical transition.

One of the first projects I worked on was called the 3:00 AM Guide, which was a breastfeeding guide with advice gathered from mothers in our

"

community. It was never published because the funders in public health didn't agree with some of the content — like acknowledging that breast-feeding can hurt! They refused to uphold their end of the partnership and I learned important lessons — to always be responsible for our own dissemination, to hold as many of the purse strings as you can, and to acknowledge that power imbalances exist even in "partnerships", which can be infuriating.

In 2009, we developed Trade HERizons, a program designed to increase the number of women in skilled trades on PEI. I led a team that collaborated with our community, government, private sector, educational institutions, and tradeswomen to address barriers women face in all aspects of the trades sector. It was amazing work And I got to do all the things I love, including using research and evidence to create a model for improving gender equity in the trades.

It was hard work but also fun and rewarding. About five years after we started Trade HERizons, a woman from the first group came to my office to show me her last pay stub of the year. She had more taken off in payroll deductions that year than she made on Social Assistance before she started Trade HERizons. Our model of supporting women to transition from poverty to a sustainable livelihood using trades as the vehicle was working! I will never forget how proud I was that day — both of her and of what we were collectively creating.

When we started Trade HERizons, the province was on track to see an equal number of men and women in the trades in 276 years. By 2017, through so much combined effort, our researcher was able to estimate that we're now on track to see that number equalize in 45 years. In less than ten years, we cut 231 years off the march to gender equality in the trades sector on PEI. How does that not get your juices flowing!?

And yet, as exciting as this is, there is still so much work to be done. Retention in the trades sector is dismal because of harassment, sexism, wage inequality, and the lack of job opportunities (despite a shortage of skilled labour) — the trades sector being a welcoming space for women is still a long way off. I am still proud that Trade HERizons continues though, and of the folks who continue this march toward equity.

By 2015, I was feeling burnt out. We wrapped up *Paths to Prosperity: A*

Community Response to Poverty. Over the three years, I led a team of researchers that included the local university, organizational staff, and a dozen subject matter experts, incorporating both women living in poverty and women experiencing the weight of broken systems. It was inspiring to see our subject matter experts build their confidence, make new community connections, and overcome their nerves to present our report with its suite of recommendations to community leaders, including the Premier and caucus. But it was both difficult and amazing to delve deeply into poverty — the swirly mess of data, stories, cause and effect, intergenerational impacts, stigma, and inequality. And although it was complicated and challenging, it also seemed so simple: don't we all want to live in a world where everyone has their needs met? And don't we have enough abundance to make that happen? We also completed "A Bold Vision" in 2014, an extraordinary collaboration of five Island women's organizations where we published a book of essays featuring Canadian women leaders, hosted a national women's leadership conference, and a public event where 800 people showed up to hear these leaders speak.

While past experience had led me to assume the women I worked with all experienced sexual violence and trauma, there was a particular intensity about that fall. It was the beginning of the #MeToo and #TimesUp movements in Canada, the Jian Ghomeshi scandal broke, the Bill Cosby allegations ramped up, and in Atlantic Canada, we had the Dalhousie University Dentistry scandal, where male students were posting misogynistic comments online about women classmates. I was experiencing vicarious trauma at a magnitude that was more than I could handle. My mental health was in jeopardy and I knew I needed a change.

Luckily there were some big wins around that time: in the spring of 2015, we celebrated Canada's first federal government with gender parity in cabinet. And that fall, we rejoiced when the provincial government announced the opening of the women's reproductive health clinic and repatriation of abortion services to PEI, a win for all women and those of us who worked collaboratively to advocate and pressure the government to make the change. It was an honour to be part of the patchwork quilt of this beautiful organization that gave me so much as a kid and as a grown up. But it was time for other folks to take the work to the next level, which they've done. As a feminist organization should, Women's Network employs passionate and committed folks who continue to evolve and respond to the changing needs of its community.

Through the leaving process, I realized that the core tenet to my life's work is that I believe gender equality can solve all of the world's problems. That's it. There's still a lot of work to do, which means there are a million entry points towards reaching gender equity. I was relieved to know I could choose a different one if I wanted. For me to be a happy human, I have to do ambitious work that moves the needle, to ensure that women's voices are heard and respected. Since I left Women's Network, I've built a thriving coaching practice, supporting women to embrace their ambition, kick imposter syndrome to the curb, build businesses and make their own money, solving their own problems.

Most recently, I've written a book called *She Rules: What You Didn't Know is Holding You Back in Business*. In it, I talk about why the business world doesn't always feel good or work for women. Spoiler alert: it's because it was created for men, inspired by military strategy, and supported by a woman at home doing everything else.

SARA ROACH LEWIS
UNSUNG HERO

In 1986, when I was appointed by Premier Joseph Ghiz to chair the PEI Advisory Council on the Status of Women, little did I realize how it would become a lifelong pursuit of equality for women. Working with Premier Ghiz, who was also the minister responsible for the Status of Women, was a dynamic experience, because he had a genuine interest in improving the status of women in the province; he understood discrimination. He had faced it personally during the election campaign he had just won, where a whisper campaign began that a person of Lebanese descent should not become Premier.

From the very beginning, we had open and frank discussions around this. We were both very surprised by the Council's tiny budget, offering only a one-room facility, two part-time staff and a shared phone, all to-talling less than $30,000 per year. The position of Chairperson was not funded, nor were the nine women who made up the Council.

During much of my time working with women in the province, I worked as a volunteer. Peter, my spouse, had the habit of replying, "How much is this one going to cost?" He referred to this each time a new challenge came along; the position as Chair of the Council was no different.

At a provincial budget planning meeting for the Council in 1986, with the Premier and Andy Wells from the Finance Department, we agreed on increases to the Council budget for the staff to become full time at better rates of pay, thus increasing the operational budget. It was important that the wages reflected local salaries for similar work in the community. The following year, the Council opened a new accessible office on Great George Street where we included a feminist lending library, board room, computers, and offices for permanent and project staff. Senator Percy Downe was a staff person in the Premier's office at the time and he worked with the Public Works Department to ensure the new office on Great George Street, was leased by government. Local businesses provided in-kind donations for the office furnishings. With the help of Madrine Ferris from the Transportation Department we went to a government storage of surplus furniture and found a wonderful old pine board room table. Cupboards and shelving were purchased for the new library.

In addition to women becoming more visible and effective, my goal was to anchor the processes of Council in legislation rather than an Order-in-Council. During our discussion about a formal review, I remember telling the Premier how insecure the Council felt when Cabinet could vote to eliminate it altogether at any Cabinet meeting. One staff person had an interesting quote we all used when talking about the need for legislation. She often said, "On any given Thursday, we could be cancelled," as Thursdays were Cabinet meeting days. Luckily, Premier Ghiz agreed to fund a review and appointed Dr. Elizabeth Percival, a professor at UPEI and former Chairperson of the Council, to lead the Review Committee. Lawyer Marlene Clark, who had senior management experience in government, joined a representative group of women from around the province. They held hearings Island-wide and collected great new ideas from many women who emphatically endorsed the need to keep the Council and strengthen its structure. Marlene drafted the legislation, as recommended by the Review Committee. And on International Women's Day, March 8, 1989, The Status of Women Advisory Council Act was tabled in the legislature by Premier Ghiz and received Royal assent in July 1989.

In subsequent years, the Council became more secure. This became very important when right-wing women, pro-life lobbyists and men's rights groups, opposed to the Council's feminist policies, became more vocal and visible over the years. Although they have publicly lobbied the government to disband the Council, that would never be an easy task because of the legislation.

The emergence of the organized, right-wing, small "c" conservative women's group on PEI meant there was a push for maintaining the status quo or the traditional values, whereas the liberal and social justice feminists focused on reforms through political action and legal reforms of democracy through their support for the Canadian Charter of Rights and Freedoms. To the liberal feminist, a just law applies to both men and women equally. This "second wave" became a women's movement in Canada and was a grassroots social action movement by women who saw the need to reform all government systems to create a true social justice, thereby effectively ending the notion of male supremacy.

One particular incident where the formal review of the Council and subsequent legislation came in handy was when the Council applied for funding under a federal employment development program. As a result of increasing requests for information — some said as many as fifty per week — a proposal had been developed to establish a computerized database of information and a lending library, serving to improve access to statistics and research of interest to those working to improve the status of women. Progressive Conservative MP Tom McMillian had been stalling in his approval of our application, and bureaucrats could not understand or explain the long delay, so the Council's Vice-Chairperson, Eileen Best and I set up a meeting to discuss the project with him.

Eileen Best was also a Progressive Conservative and a donor to the Party, so felt free to share her opinions about the need for the Council's project. She emphasized that its success depended on the computers and training for staff, which were stated goals of the federal program. Tom questioned whether the ACSW (Advisory Council on the Status of Women) was still needed because he had been lobbied by right-wing women who wanted it abolished. After we explained that a province-wide review had just been done and legislation passed, we moved on with our agenda for the meeting.

Tom seemed surprised to see both Eileen and me at the meeting and spent some time speaking to Eileen about her historic home in Cardigan, after which we had a brief discussion about the project and left the meeting on friendly terms. Afterwards, Tom must have agreed that the application from the Council was not a partisan Liberal project. Eileen and I were both known to be members of different political parties; what we did share was a common interest in seeking equality for women. We received approval for the funding to develop a computerized lending library not long after.

The first people to request a meeting with me as Chairperson of the Council were Lyle Brehaut and Lorna Gallant from the PEI Rape and Sexual Assault Crisis Centre. Their request was to be able to make a presentation to the Council as a whole. We agreed that they could have an hour at our next meeting. Lyle was very well prepared and had written a brief to circulate to members after her presentation.

It was often believed that rape and sexual assault did not happen on PEI. It was not discussed publicly and very few incidents were reported to police. In 1981, a gang rape court case came to the attention of the public and caused a small group of women to found the PEI Rape and Sexual Assault Crisis Centre and set up a 24 hr hot-line; it had become apparent that contrary to popular belief, rape and childhood sexual violence did happen here. Lyle became the first coordinator and worked in that role for fifteen years.

Following the presentation, Council requested permission to publish the paper in order for more policy makers to understand the needs of the PEI Rape and Sexual Assault Crisis Centre. The Council gave the writing credit to Lyle, as the author, for the excellent work and named

Lyle Brehaut answering the Rape and Sexual Assault Crisis
phone line; early 1980's

the paper Believe Her. The basic issue women were facing was that they were not taken seriously, And I even remember MLAs who questioned whether or not the assaults were true. The Council released the report to the media, did a mass printing of it and circulated it Island-wide, where public education and support could begin. The Rape Crisis Centre was given dozens of copies to use for their public education purposes.

Becky Tramley, Executive Assistant, ACSW

Council was happy to take part in this partnership, because few women's organizations had the funding to do this kind of distribution. The Council's minutes and mail were coordinated by Executive Assistant Becky Tramley, and all mail-outs were donated in-kind to by the PEI government postal service. At some point over the last thirty years Council is now required to pay its own postage, within a budget that has not grown much beyond the 1987 increase.

One time, we were contacted by

the media to respond to a court conviction against Island MLA Peter Pope. Council had been discussing his case, when he was charged with physical assault against a Summerside woman. We made the decision to call for his resignation if he was found guilty or plead guilty; violence against women is a serious crime that had for so long gone under-reported. By calling for his resignation after he pled guilty, we wanted to send the message that violence against women would not be tolerated by anyone, no matter their status in society. Assaults would not be swept under the rug. After a loud public outcry over the course of several weeks in the media, Pope resigned as MLA, having been found intoxicated in public after assaulting his victim. We emphasized with the media that alcohol and drug use did not excuse violence against women, and that violence is a choice made by perpetrators that cannot be excused.

In partnership with LEAF (the Legal Education Action Fund) and NAWL (the National Association of Women and the Law), the Council took part in the annual Person's Day Breakfast to raise funds for local LEAF activities. The event was held in Charlottetown in October each year, and prominent women from the community were asked to dress in period costume of the 1920s. Five women, Canada's Famous Five, were the leaders of the campaign to legally challenge the practice of appointing only men to the Senate of Canada. One Island woman, Ann Sherman, became one of the Famous Five because of her long record of volunteerism and commitment to the women's movement. Lawyers Linda Gaudet, Beverly Mills Stetson, Delores Crane, and I as Chair of the ACSW, welcomed guests at the door while trying to stay in character at the first year of this event.

Dianne sits at the monument recognizing Canada's "Famous Five"

The Council also made forays into education. In partnership with the UPEI Department of Education and Psychology & PEI Departments of Industry and Education, the Student Attitude Survey project began its work in 1985, publishing a report titled, "High School and Beyond" in 1988. The study, which began years earlier, examined course selections and future plans of PEI high school students. The ten recommendations were all directed to the Department Education, with many of them being implemented immediately. Others however, would take years to fully see results, such as the recommendation to improve the occupational opportunities of girls in mathematics and science in order to lessen the effects of sex role stereotyping in enrolment. This recommendation spurred the Council and community to put together a project called, "PEI Women Do Math and Science". I remember one poster from that time that listed jobs and above the list it read: *"Dropping Math? Say Goodbye to 100 Jobs."*

The three years I spent as Chairperson of the Council were years of structural change for the council itself, and were also a time when several key public issues became major issues for women. This included the Supreme Court's decision to strike down the restrictive abortion laws in Canada in 1988. The Canadian Advisory Council on the Status of Women still existed at the time, and their federal leadership led the national response and provided information to the public aimed at ensuring understanding and the impact on women's equality. Locally, the Canadian Abortion Rights Action League's spokesperson, Dr. Alice Crook, led the public discussions on PEI. The PEI Advisory Council's policy spoke about access to reproductive services and prevention.

While the Supreme Court decision was pending on the *R vs Morgentaler* case, the PEI Council knew we must prepare for either the Court upholding women's equality rights or non-consideration of them. Prior to that 1988 decision, Council developed a policy paper that represented the opinions expressed in past Council's statements and current opinions of the Council members. It was not an easy process and took many rounds of discussion. The Pro-Choice Policy was adopted; however, as a sign of the times, one woman chose to abstain from the vote. I was intrigued by her reasoning: "I don't want my husband to know I am pro-choice because our family is Roman Catholic." Therefore, the influence of the Church meant the policy was not a unanimous one. When the Court struck down the restrictive abortion laws as unconstitutional, we were prepared to make public our policy statement.

The PEI Council had decided the major issues for Island women was both prevention and access. Our pro-choice policy and the lack of funding for reproductive health services drew our lines for the lobbying efforts. They began in 1988 and ended when Premier Wade MacLaughlan's government made the commitment to open the first clinic at Prince County Hospital in 2016, after thirty years of dispute between women and their government.

On many issues, the Council worked in partnership with individual expert women who donated their time when bigger challenges came along. Often I would call an ad hoc meeting of local experts and during the discussions, we would share opinions for Council deliberation and decision making, and the experts would assist us to map the way forward.

The First Ministers of the country released a constitutional accord developed at a long-weekend meeting at Meech Lake in Québec. Premier Ghiz and Minister Wayne Cheverie attended for PEI. The document became known as the *Meech Lake Accord*, and the assessments that came in from across the country after experts had studied the documents agreed that it was flawed, and had the potential to negatively impact women's equality rights. Finding a flaw in the constitutional Accord wasn't exactly a shock. I called together a committee of legal experts and we agreed to set up a meeting with the Premier. Section Fifteen, which covered women's equality, was being made subservient to a proposed new section of the Charter, which intended to bring Québec into the constitution, as it had not yet signed on to the Charter of Rights and Freedoms.

At our meeting with Premier Ghiz, he listened intently and took notes. As he had previously agreed, he made the phone call to Prime Minister Brian Mulroney and made the case for the rights of women. At a follow-up meeting, the Premier said, "I'm sorry, there is no 'egregious error' in the Accord and if we open it to fix this, it will all unravel." We left the Premier's office, totally demoralized, and struggled to plan our next steps. However, he did agree to raise the issue at the next First Minister's conference. Attending the meeting about the constitution with the Premier that day were

Daphne Dumont, representing the Legal Education Action Fund (LEAF), Beverly Mills Stetson, of the National Association of Women and the Law, along with Heather Irving and myself, from the Advisory Council on the Status of Women.

In the community, the grassroots groups kicked back into action. A small group of women convened and decided to put together an information campaign about the Accord. In drawing the cover diagram for the information brochure, we all had a contribution to make. The crux of the diagram was a drowning woman with a ball and chain around her ankle, and in order to provide hope it showed one weak link. The distribution list for the brochure went to all Island women's organizations and to the media. Pressure began to build on PEI and across Canada, as Indigenous leaders were also affronted by the Accord and wanted a specific clause outlining Indigenous rights. I don't think I had ever heard the word 'egregious' before the *Meech Lake Accord*, but now I was hearing it in the news daily from all across the country.

In order to develop a broader information campaign, we needed funds. We decided to hold an information night, called The *Meech Lake Screech*, at the Rodd Royalty in West Royalty, which was Chaired by Dr. Elizabeth Percival. National board member of LEAF, Daphne Dumont, explained that LEAF was accustomed to acting as a legal watchdog and took select cases to the Supreme Court of Canada, with the goal of attaining precedent-setting decisions under the equality clause of the Charter of Rights and Freedoms. She was a wonderful guest speaker, and walked us through the constitution and the potential impact of the Accord. Her final words to the large audience were, "No wonder women won't buy the 'don't worry, just trust us'. You can see now we also had equally expert legal advice, telling us that there was plenty to worry about."

On the silent auction table and at the event, patrons could buy rocks from Meech Lake for $5.00, t-shirts were sold, and the grand prize for the raffle was a vacation for two at the government owned Meech Lake Resort. A call came in from a bureaucrat from Ottawa questioning how we could promise that prize when the Resort was not open to the public. My answer was "Trust us!" The much-needed funds were raised and were put to good use when we were asked by the Premier to identify one woman scholar to come to the Island to appear before the Legislative Committee assigned to hold public hearings before taking a vote to ratify the accord. The consensus was to nominate Toronto lawyer and LEAF member, Mary Eberts.

DELEGATION TELLS PREMIER OF MEECH LAKE ACCORD CONCERNS

Premier Joe Ghiz meets Tuesday with a delegation of women concerned about the possible loss of women's rights under the Meech Lake constitutional accord. From LEFT: Beverly Mills-Stetson, representing the P.E.I. caucus of the National Association of Women and the Law; Daphne Dumont, representing the Legal Education Action Fund, Heather Irving and Dianne Porter, representing the Advisory Council on the Status of Women. (2-9-87-19a-8)

Delegation meeting with Premier Ghiz to discuss the Meech
Lake Accord

The Advisory Council on the Status of Women was the first group to appear before the special committee of the legislature, and with the help of our ad hoc legal committee we had a pretty solid argument to make. It was just about to begin when I noticed Honourable Wayne Cheverie walk into the room with the committee. My gut reaction was to feel sabotaged. How could the committee hold open and unbiased hearings when one of the Accord's designers sat on the committee? I saw a conflict of interest and called them out on it. After looking from one to another the committee rose and left the room for a break. When they returned they simply said they took a vote and they wanted Wayne Cheverie to stay on the committee. In fact, the media described it later as a Kangaroo Court.

We charged ahead with our submission, and a few weeks later constitutional lawyer Mary Eberts appeared before the committee. She was the only out of town witness who was not met at the airport or taken out to dinner by the Special Committee. Women were obviously seen as the opposition rather than as collaborators. Meeting with Mary on the evening she arrived, the ad hoc committee of women were able to brief her on the personalities around that committee table and some of the local issues that had been raised by other groups. Mary wanted to be sure she understood the proclivities of each member so she could better approach her answers to their questions.

In the end, after many Islanders and groups made presentations, the Legislative Committee recommended a formal vote to ratify and support the *Meech Lake Accord*. One by one, the other provinces voted the same way. When the Accord was to be voted on at the Manitoba legislature, it was the last province to try to ratify the Accord. In order to be included in the Charter of Rights and Freedoms, the *Meech Lake Accord* required unanimous consent by the provinces. One sole Manitoba MLA dissenter stood with his eagle feather and said, "NO!" Indigenous leader and MLA Elijah Harper had scuttled it. He accomplished what feminists could not and protected equality rights for women as guaranteed in the Canadian Charter of Rights and Freedoms, standing firmly for Indigenous rights to be specifically protected in the constitution and the Accord that had left them out.

The First Minister's Accord failed. While it would not be the last attempt, we all learned something very important from that experience: it was vital to be forever vigilant of government actions on constitutional

Opening of the ACSW office on Great George Street in 1987
L-R: Bob Crocket, Deputy Minister of Labour, Premier Ghiz, Dianne Porter,
Chairperson and Rachna Gilmour, Vice Chairperson.

matters, in order to protect equality rights outlined in the Canadian Charter of Rights and Freedoms.

Stemming from Council meetings and consultations, there were often times when briefs were released to the media, or presented to the PEI legislature. Other times letters were written to organizations or businesses, but the Council continued to make its voice heard. Members of the Advisory Council on the Status of Women were often invited to speak at schools, women's gatherings, and events. Following my three years at the Council, we produced a three year report called "Diversity, Vitality and Change" which documented the hundreds of activities and pressures put on a small group of mostly volunteer women, to speak out for equality for Island women.

With some excess Council funds and a generous in-kind donation from an Atlantic polling firm, the Council decided to do a "Survey on Women's Health" and violence against women and reproductive health were included. The survey results of Islanders' opinions reflected the Pro-Choice policy of the Council. One of the findings that became quite contentious in the media was that a large percentage of Islanders who identified as Roman Catholic were pro-choice. The reasoning they gave was that even though they held a pro-life view personally, it did not extend to others of different religions who may make different decisions about their own beliefs and their body's integrity. It was common during public debates in the 1980s for the media to divide the debate equally by religion and the Island was 50% Catholic at the time. Once and for all this question was answered by the health survey, and no longer could the public, the media, or governments say that half of the province's population were anti-abortion.

The release of the entire Health Survey in 1988 generated interest by government and members of the Legislature. Within government, departmental briefing notes from key civil servants in health and social services were updated after the Morgentaler decision, then updated again with the new Health Survey results. Politicians received up-to-date information, but it was their own decision to follow or not to follow the expert advice.

A public debate and letter writing campaign informed the Legislature;

however, a resolution was introduced in the Legislature to limit women's right to choose on the Island. Legislators' speeches were given and one by one they stood to vote against women's right to abortion on PEI, even though there was no longer a criminal law preventing abortions. The resolution passed, "to allow abortion, but only to protect the health of the mother." When the resolution passed, the Council members who were in the gallery met with the media and immediately asked for "reproductive health services for women, including funding for abortion for "mothers whose health was at risk". Of course there was never any intention by the Government to provide those services for women's reproductive health at that time.

The first time Island women received Health PEI paid abortion services for out of province hospital abortions was in 1996. It would take until 2016, when in-province abortion services and other reproductive health care concerns were finally covered under the PEI Health Care Act, but only after a legal challenge of government policy by women. A shocking twenty-four years after the Supreme Court decision struck down restrictive abortion laws, the Wade MacLaughlin government established the Women's Wellness Centre at the Prince County Hospital.

The history of women's reproductive health became an important Island issue from the time when approval and legalization was given of the birth control pill in the 1960's. PEI had a branch of Planned Parenthood brought to the Island by Janet Dale, when she travelled the island along with a small group of women whose goal was to provide health information to girls and women, in particular around reproductive rights. To fund the group's activities, Janet and her partner Alan Preston set up a flower shop called Hearts and Flowers. When Planned Parenthood stopped operating on the Island, Alan purchased this social initiative and the Hearts and Flowers we know today is one and the same.

In 1986, the aging and homogeneous Advisory Council on the Status of Women membership, with an average age of seventy-three, was a concern to both Premier Ghiz and to our Council itself. Over the course of the next three years we were able to create diversity by age, race, religion, ethnic origin, and profession as positions expired and new appointments were made. The Council welcomed the new perspective: Rikki Schock was appointed as the first Indigenous woman, Rachna Gilmour, an Island children's author and new visible minority Canadian, was appointed as Vice-Chairperson, and Asifa Rhaman, a member of the Immigrant Women's Association, became a member of the council. The dynamics of the Council changed as did the priorities, all for the embetterment of the status of Island women.

While the Council group forged ahead, sometimes there were unfortunate events, and one such incident that occurred caused both myself and the Premier great concern. A small group of non-Council members had made posters of a local man, calling him out as a "rapist", and affixed them to electric poles all over his neighbourhood. Immediately, the media and the police began investigating. When I got to the office that day, however, I learned that the Council paper posters, which were available to the public for free, had been used by the group. They simply printed their poster on the back of ours — thus implicating the Council. We were pursued by the media for comment, and I was called in to a meeting with Premier Ghiz as the Minister Responsible for the Status of Women; it was decided that I meet immediately with the police to answer their questions.

At the time, I had no idea who had been involved or why. But over the course of the next few days, it became clear who had intended to compromise the Council. That individual, who lost my respect and trust, resigned. *A Globe and Mail* reporter with a camera came to the office to request an interview and after an 'off-the-record chat' with me, he left without a story to tell. I was certainly not going to comment on an incident under investigation by police. Furthermore, my children were young at the time, and I was genuinely fearful of a backlash against them, as teachers and classmates sometimes made negative comments. This time would likely prove to be no exception.

In March of 1989, the Council released a report on intimate partner violence called, *The Black and Blue Paper: Questions to Consider*. It was released when the provincial election was called and our women's campaign included a full blue page in *The Guardian* that contained the black diagram of a target and the large black lettering saying "Target Abuse". *Black and Blue* brochures were distributed across the Island and the campaign served as an educational opportunity in addition to political lobbying.

One of the last public events as Chairperson that I attended was the gathering in front of the government buildings on Rochford Street in Charlottetown. The Montréal Massacre had just occurred, where fourteen bright, young female engineering students were gunned down and killed by a disgruntled man who was against the presence of women in engineering at École Polytechnique de Montréal. The rally was demanding that the Premier make a public statement on the topic of violence against women and girls. I attended the gathering with my two young daughters, and all I could do that day was clutch their hands as tears streamed down my face. I was unable to speak to the gathering that day. However, the Council's Executive Director, Houston Stewart did speak out very strongly on our behalf, as did representatives of other women's organizations. It was hard to believe that the public discussion in the media actually questioned if this could be considered violence against women. Attending the yearly memorial service on December 6th that honours those lost women, and other women who have lost their lives due to intimate partner violence, has become an annual activity for both my daughters and I. They live in Ottawa where there is a small stone-made memorial in a city park on Elgin Street, and large candle-light gatherings are organized there each year.

The impact that my service work and public life had on family life, even as I continued in my management role at the orthodontic office, caused a significant time squeeze. After three years of this demanding volunteer work, I decided it was time to change gears. I moved on from the Council and enrolled in courses, part-time at UPEI studying Public Administration and doing my office work during the children's school hours. It freed up more time after school to spend with the children and their growing needs and activities, and created a more flexible schedule for the family. There was a certain controversy around my decision to move on, and some women who were involved in the 'rapist poster campaign' spun it in their favour. For years, I felt a backlash from the women who supported that renegade group.

A few years following my time at the Advisory Council on the Status of Women, a new Executive Director was hired. Lisa Murphy, who stayed in the job for nearly thirty years, created excellent policies with Council members, worked exceptionally well with community groups, and was constantly providing excellent information to the public and Council. She withstood many attacks on the Council and bravely fought to keep the structure and mandate positive — even when the pressure was coming from within government itself. She served with many councils representing diversity across the province.

UNSUNG HERO
LISA MURPHY

I had just graduated with a Political Science degree at UPEI and finished my year as President of the Student Union when I took a position as Communications Coordinator at the provincial Advisory Council on the Status of Women. It is hard to believe, but that was thirty plus years ago and the start of a career working for women's equality.

The political science study and degree gave me a historical and contemporary framework of the powerful and perpetual process of upheaval and change. I needed that framework when looking at gender equality. My work at the Status of Women was in presenting information that a lot of people did not want to see, or that people did not believe. For me, my job in communications was a fast lesson in promoting equity to disparate groups. We seemed to be in a constant state of making our case; in educating everyone, internally, from our own Government-appointed board of directors, elected members of the legislature including the Minister Responsible and Premier, to Department staff, and externally to the public. I learned a lot about the politics of this province, how it relates to the country, and how we could achieve positive and sustained influence on the status of women.

At the Status of Women, our job was to point out where the province wasn't doing so well to improve the status of women, but not be too loud. It was a fine line between drawing attention to problem areas that needed fixing by the Government and motivating the powers that be to make the necessary corrections for all Islanders. A challenging arm's length position that left us additionally thwarted by receiving operating funds from that same Government.

The global women's movement in the late 80s and 90s was important and thrilling, and our days on PEI were also filled with protest, research, writing, presentations, proposals, and lobby efforts. Markers of success for me came from the positive difference we were making, albeit quietly and over time. Markers of failure came from sustained funding shortages, from seeing the dark side fear of them losing privilege, and from seeing policies and politics remain fixed that kept barriers in front of women just trying to get by or to get out of a violent situation. Advancements on raising the status of women were possible only with combined efforts of determined, like-minded equality seekers.

I also went for the job because I was unsuccessfully dealing with several years of violence and sexual violation, and discovered there was little recourse for me and many girls and women like me. The inability of the community and justice system to handle such incidents was staggering. Victim blaming and the personal nature of the crimes (he said/she said) meant women got very little support and even less retribution. Without political reform, I knew that entitled men who violate women will suffer no consequences and walk away. I knew I could and should work on this issue.

So, I took that first job at the Advisory Council on the Status of Women in 1990, and in two short years became Executive Director. I was proud of our small and mighty team. There were many achievements in influencing policy and programs and showcasing women in all areas of life on PEI, despite inadequate funds to fulfill the Council's lofty legal Government mandate.

The only way we were going to have success in helping advance equality, and equal opportunity for girls and women in PEI, was to collaborate with women of influence in communities across the Island. I used my leadership position and that of the council board members to coordinate large provincial working committees on specific areas of need that in turn could then apply for grant money for equality initiatives. It was a way of networking that brought women together in goals and action.

As Executive Director, I saw success in collaboration. My memories are full of teams of dedicated women working together from the ground up. My memories are of the multitude of Women and Art projects that profiled female artists and raised funds for women in organizations working against unchecked violence in our Island homes. My memories are of seeing the bright eyes and hopeful hearts of grade eight girls meeting PEI women in careers in medicine, engineering, science, and math fields. My memories are of creating bright purple ribbons to mark the Annual Purple Ribbon Campaign, an initiative that brought municipal and provincial parties together in effort to educate all Islanders about the facts surrounding abuse and violence against women by men. My memories are of the major political reform of the Maintenance Enforcement system when Premier Catherine Callbeck followed through on her 1993 election promise to implement our committee report recommendations.

The PEI Advisory Council on the Status of Women is an existing PEI Government agency which in my opinion is provided with limited resources to do its work. I found the work at the Council both exhausting and rewarding, a nod to committee work structure, constant diplomacy with opposition, and stubborn resolve. After twenty-three plus years of work at the Council, I reflect on my work and that of my colleagues, many of whom are dear friends, and cherish even the smallest steps forward. Advancements where Island girls, women, and their communities recognized that they are worthy and deserve equality and equality of opportunity that boys and men enjoy, things like equal pay, safety from violence, and control over their own reproductive rights.

I am delighted that Dianne Porter, a former PEI Advisory Council on the Status of Women Chairperson, and an effective equality agitator, has worked with me on so many challenging projects over the years. I am humbled to have been asked by her about my days in the women's movement on PEI, and I am deeply honoured to have them included in this book.

Lisa, now retired, is a visual artist and maker of high-end jewelry and hand-sewn leather crafts. She makes her home in Charlottetown and is the proud mother of two strong daughters following in her footsteps.

LISA MURPHY
UNSUNG HERO

As is the case with government, new Ministers Responsible for the Status of Women are appointed from time to time and it is during these times that priorities shift. One Minister bowed to pressure from the right-wing group named R.E.A.L. (Realistic, Equal, Active, for Life) women and their pro-family male supporters. It wasn't long before there was a physical move of the Advisory Council on the Status of Women into a much smaller, less visible space. The library was dismantled, and staff found themselves hidden from public view. The appointment of a right-wing anti-feminist to the Council was made by one Minister who seemed to misunderstand the basic premise; the promotion of equality was the mandate, not challenging equality gains made by women.

One Council Chairperson who followed me a few years later stood out as an excellent spokesperson and effective negotiator. Anne Nicholson brought a determination and light warmhearted spirit to the Council, and it is because of dedicated people like her that the Council continues to thrive and to do excellent work. Anne has had a distinguished career, and has held many important positions in our Island community.

Once a year, past-Chairpersons of the Advisory Council on the Status of Women join for a session called the Chair's Circle. This meeting offers experienced opinions on current equality issues, and our discussion often becomes part of the internal Council conversation around policies. Anne Nicholson, Lisa Murphy and I had all discussed the creation of the Circle and the lost expertise once the terms were ended. In later years, I was happy to see this assembly come to fruition, and it continues to be a valuable resource to the current Chairperson.

UNSUNG HERO
ANNE NICHOLSON

I grew up in Montreal and moved to Prince Edward island when I was nineteen years old. The Island and Islanders themselves made me feel that I belonged, and so for forty-seven years, I have made this place my home. I knew I was a feminist from an early age: my mother Leila Nicholson was a great role model, and my father Ross was a big supporter.

However, my feminist convictions heightened when, at age twenty-two, I was sexually assaulted. I went through the painfully difficult and humiliating process known as the "rape kit" and reported this traumatic incident to the police. Afterwards, I became more politically active, circulating petitions, attending "Take Back the Night" marches, and participated in many feminist workshops, festivals, and events.

I began volunteering at the PEI Rape Crisis Centre, and later worked there. I witnessed the impact of sexual assault on many women who were victims, including young girls who had suffered sexual abuse from a young age. These experiences deepened my convictions, and many have framed my paid and unpaid work ever since that time.

Over the years, I have served on several boards addressing family violence prevention, including the Premier's Action Committee on Family Violence Prevention and Anderson House. As the Family Violence Prevention coordinator in Kings County, I initiated projects and programs addressing relationship violence with youth. S.A.V.E., or Students Against Violence Everywhere, became a program at Montague and Morell High Schools that involved students in designing violence prevention programs with their peers; "Yes 4 Youth" brought people working with young people together to ensure violence prevention was part of every program; "E.S.P."(Equal, Safe and Proud) was group training for young girls to encourage self-esteem in a supportive group setting.

In the early 1990s I was appointed Chairperson of the PEI Advisory Council on the Status of Women and worked alongside Lisa Murphy, the Executive Director. We travelled the Island to consult with women to learn about their experiences and priorities. I was also able to bring Island issues to national joint-meetings of other Advisory Councils from across Canada. These were times of sharing and learning from one another and I always came back from those meetings invigorated and determined to work even harder for issues important to Island women.

A few years later, I became a commissioner of the PEI Human Rights Commission and later became the Chairperson where some intriguing cases came forward from the public. I adjudicated cases and worked for many changes to the Human Rights Act. I worked for the protection of gay rights, gender identity and gender expression, which soon became protected by the Human Rights Act. For several years, I was employed by the Community Legal Information Association to help seniors navigate their legal needs by producing information booklets. I also spent time staffing the telephone information line, and directed callers to legal professionals when needed.

Since 2019 I have worked as a Justice of the Peace for the Victims of Family Violence Act. My role is to hear applications for Emergency Protection Orders (EPOs) by victims of family violence. While on call, I review the applications which come by phone directly to me anytime, day or night. I decide their eligibility and swear in testimony from the applicant before putting into effect an EPO, which may include granting sole use of the home and temporary custody of any children as well as orders for the respondent to stay away from the victim, their home, family, and workplace for up to ninety days. It is heart wrenching to hear the stories and realize that so many people on PEI live in fear for themselves and their children every day. While it is good to be able to offer some respite to victims while they look for long-term solutions, it has taken its toll on me, and it is hard not to dwell on the violence and fear that victims often face.

The COVID-19 pandemic has illuminated many areas where women have lost ground in the struggle for equality; however, I remain optimistic that new generations, both women and men, will step forward to be role models for others. With my encouragement and support, the fight continues.

ANNE NICHOLSON
UNSUNG HERO

Anne Nicholson, Lisa Murphy and Dianne attend
THE VAGINA MONOLOGUES

In 1990, two years after I had left the Council, Premier Ghiz again asked if I would advise the government. His request this time was that I develop a PEI Women's Secretariat, to advise on policy development inside government and to act as the Executive Director. I agreed to a one year contract and I believed we could accomplish the task to create the organization in that time frame.

The culture of working inside the bureaucracy, however, was unexpectedly nasty and competitive for me. There was unease within the civil service, which seemed to stem from the work being done by the Office of Government Reform, which had been established to bring about the changes requested by the Ghiz Cabinet, and to meet new financial pressures during a global recession. It was a very stressful environment across government, as programs were being changed or eliminated and staff were being moved, some were losing jobs, and others were offered early retirement.

The Secretariat staff was not spared the stressful impact of reform, and their concerns could not be answered by myself or the Minister Roberta Hubley because the reforms were in development and unknown at that time. It was the first year of our organization and holding on to funds became a big issue — but regardless of the stress, we were finding our way. At the end of this one year contract with the government though, I was totally burnt out. Luckily, I had met other public servants across the country who were experiencing the same stresses in leadership and we were able to support one another. Some of these supporters I had met at a government management training retreat, and we are still friends to this day.

In order to do the work of providing the feminist viewpoint to government, we were very fortunate to have a highly skilled policy analyst at the Secretariat, Louise Polland. No matter what question I asked about government policy she replied, "I track that". The Premier had requested that I attend meetings with Deputy Ministers during the Government Reform process and for one such meeting, Louise had prepared a financial briefing note as a reference for me. With the briefing note in hand, I could back up the Secretariat's recommendations for change.

Following the first meeting, I was asked about my briefing notes by other Deputies and I gladly shared them. First, I had Louise prepare contact information about herself to take credit for her work, something that had formerly been frowned upon. From then onward Louise became a visible, important, well respected policy analyst within the Secretariat, and beyond that, throughout the whole of the public service. She was often seconded to do important policy work in other departments. One such time, she worked with the PEI Legislature to research and draft a report on the

Maritime Union. Whenever I have the opportunity to introduce Louise to others I always say, "Louise is the most intelligent person I know." This is just another example of how the feminist community on PEI continues to collaborate and celebrate our strengths.

UNSUNG HERO
LOUISE POLLAND

I was born in Berkeley, California. and al-though I have been away for fifty years and don't intend to return, there are still dear friends and family there. Having never fit in, and feeling that the place was full of phonies, I planned to leave after high school. When I was eleven years old, I read the *Anne* series by Lucy Maud Montgomery, and fell in love with the PEI landscape; I was hooked.

My parents encouraged me to go to uni-versity, and I decided to attend Prince of Wales College, which had just become the University of Prince Edward Island. It was a wonderful place to study and learn, and I made good friends with whom I am still close. During that time, I also became a member of the Baha'i Faith. I became a landed immigrant in university, and a citizen as soon as I could manage it. After working for a while at various jobs on PEI, I went to Montreal to go to the Université de Montréal. After a year there, I switched to Con-cordia where I could study while working full-time. I began to specialize in Biology, and I went deeper and deeper into the microcosm of the cell. But I was terrible at the actual laboratory work, so I followed my interest and began a career in science writing, interviewing researchers and putting their words into English — or French, as the case might be. I missed living on PEI, though, and eventually I decided to return.

Several months after returning to PEI, a job was advertised for a policy analyst with the provincial government. I applied for the job, got it, and became enthralled with policy work. To me, the point of the job was to gather as much information as possible on whatever the issue might be and to condense it into the fundamental facts. It also required a good deal of intuitive thinking as well.

I believe that one of our most important things we can do for each other as fellow human beings is to witness the joys and tribulations of others, and to be ready to help when assistance is needed. I believe we are all policy analysts, struggling as we go through life to find the meaning that lies within.

LOUISE POLLARD
UNSUNG HERO

The first annual report of the Women's Secretariat described the Strategic Influence Model, which we had developed during that first year as our model of operation and placed the organization as a central agency. We felt it was important to structure it within the public service as partners with government departments, and to work with them in order to reach government goals to better profile the experiences of Island girls and women. Working in isolation, connected to the Department of Labour, and trying to influence decisions in the greater cultural arena had not been a successful government strategy; change was required.

The Guiding Principles for the Women's Secretariat were developed internally at our staff meetings and written by Lee Bartley, the Communications Coordinator. We were proud when this first annual report was tabled in the Legislature and captured our work, and it became a guiding document.

The principles at the Secretariat began with staff applying a gender sensitive perspective which encouraged constantly asking: "Is gender a factor in this policy or program, given the circumstances that exist?" The aim was to incorporate women's values and work styles into the government's formalized structure, and to actively promote women in decision making. This was a critical piece of thinking at the time, as it was an era where only a handful of women were senior managers. The staff of the Secretariat and our internal partners worked collectively in order to achieve the promotion of women's views across government, mindfully adopting a win/win framework that encompassed an agreement that satisfied both sides of the issue.

This idea behind this framework is based on the philosophy that there is a third alternative — one which values and accommodates differences. Opposing viewpoints did not necessarily mean that the male view was hostile, although some individual men were. In government, seldom is an issue resolved on early attempts. The issues could be seen as a multi-step process and win/win thinking aimed to get issues resolved one step at a time.

There were three positions that the Secretariat could have adopted on any given issue. The first position was gender-neutral, where everyone was treated the same. The second was gender-separate, where women were accommodated separately. The third position was a gender-sensitive approach that allowed the Secretariat to be flexible and apply accommodations at different times and under different circumstances. Most of the time, our approach to policy recommendations was to choose to take the gender sensitive approach.

During that first year of development, the Federal, Provincial, and Territorial Ministers Responsible for the Status of Women met to consider the new financial realities for governments. The staff at the Women's Secretariat had the strategic role to play to support our Minister, the Honourable Roberta Hubley. At a joint meeting with the Canadian Ministers of Education, we learned quickly that provincial jurisdiction was a constitutional undercurrent for those in the education system. Agreed-upon statements from Federal-Provincial-Territorial meetings of Ministers are generally acted on individually in provinces across the country and are reported on at subsequent meetings. This particular meeting, unfortunately, turned out to be a complete waste of time and money for us, with PEI Education Ministry representatives coming back to the province, who did not value our work. The department refused to collaborate on issues highlighted in the joint statement. We returned devastated for PEI girls and women, as all of our carefully planned ideas had — in no uncertain terms — died. But sadly, the fight for women's equality has never been a road paved in gold. So on we marched.

A few years following that first development year of the Secretariat, the group was renamed the Inter-Ministerial Women's Secretariat, which better reflected its actual function. The Executive Directors that followed me had different priorities, as did the Ministers Responsible, however, the structure has remained over time and has become an increasingly accepted model across government. Contributions, both large and small, are still made by the Secretariat, in partnership with other departments, community groups and the Advisory Council on the Status of Women, to improve equality for girls and women in the province. The work continues.

In budget cuts in 1991, the staff of five at the Secretariat was reduced to three, and not long after that, to two. It has remained at very low staff levels since that time. There are always efforts to change the size and scope of the Secretariat, and very creative staff are able to build relationships and partnerships across government, no matter how small their budget, and in the community to ensure the voices of women are heard. Sometimes it seems that the Government wants to have the structures supporting the status of women in place, but they do not always put their money into action.

When Premier Ghiz called on me a third time, it was following my year of development of the Women's Secretariat. This time it was to join the Task Force on Quality Management, which was a six-month position. The Task Force studied best practices in other jurisdictions and many documents on quality management. Quality in management is an act of overseeing all activities and tasks that must be accomplished to maintain a desired level of excellence. It is essential that the department or program have a quality mindset. Our terms of reference from Cabinet were to recommend and advise on quality planning and assurance and quality control. Our Task Force thus immediately began the search for internal and external models.

Consultations were held with key government civil servants within the system and the final report was presented to Premier Ghiz by Chairperson Mark Belfry in 1992. Key recommendations for the Government included the need for the leadership to innovate to create future success, and for civil servants to encourage new ideas and new ways of accomplishing goals. In order to attain this, employee training in quality management principles was seen as essential by the task force. When policies and programs were developed, we believed they should not remain static but incorporate the principles of continuous improvement. In summary, the report saw the need for a government-wide policy on Quality Management, with a built-in review and reassessment period to determine if goals were being met. The idea of regularly reviewing what other jurisdictions across the country are doing is an important part of any assessment, so "best practices" that were already working in other jurisdictions could be added and form part of the PEI policy discussions. Many of these recommendations were implemented immediately, although some came up against resistance from within the public service.

With the exception of the one year at the Women's Secretariat, my years of feminist activity for women and children was as a volunteer, and as is the case with many service workers or activists, there were costs both economic and personal. With the Task Force work complete, it was my intention to return to my studies at UPEI and to put in more time at the orthodontic office. Over the next seven years, I guided our teenaged children as they learned to fly, while at the same time earning a BA in Political Science with a minor in Women's Studies at UPEI. Although I would have preferred to major in Women's Studies, the University did not and still does not offer this fundamental research area.

When my youngest daughter, Emily, graduated from high school and went off Island to study, Peter and I were facing an empty nest. After much discussion, I applied to Carleton University in Ottawa to study for a Master's Degree in Canadian Studies, with a focus on women. When I was accepted on a full scholarship, I was very grateful. I was also hired as a teacher's assistant in the first year, and a research assistant in the second. My research included an examination of all Women's Studies programs at universities across the country, to determine the existence and scope of post-graduate gender based analysis (GBA) training. I reported my findings to the Carleton University GBA Feasibility Study Committee, who were reviewing the need for a formal, continuing education certificate program for policy analysts who were already in the workforce.

The time I spent at Carleton was invigorating. With excellent professors like Dr. Katherine Arnup, the coordinator of Women's Studies, and a bright group of eager young students who met for graduate seminars, I felt truly at home. I was delighted to be included within the smaller group of brilliant young women engaging in progressive conversations about the future of Women's Studies. One interesting sidebar about my time with them at Carleton was that I learned to like red beer and blue jeans.

While studying at Carleton University, my graduate thesis focused on women in the Prince Edward Island fisheries. I conducted a follow-up study of the research about Island women in the fisheries completed by Dr. Estelle Reddin at UPEI in 1984. Because my study came fourteen years after Dr. Reddin's, my study was able to document how the world of the fisheries had changed. Due to the globalization of the economy, Canadian and provincial government reforms had created a change in the role of women in fishing families. Whereas once they were supporting the family fishing operations at home without pay and on the wharves by doing on-shore tasks, their lives were now more complex. Beginning in the 1990s, government reforms brought in changes and the women in the fisheries were being provided the initial computers and training by the Government to take over the role of keeping statistics on the catch and the boat crews. Many women joined the paid workforce on fishing boats, and others worked away from fishing in jobs such as teachers, nurses, and child care providers. Few fisher women were licensed in their own right in the lobster fishery at that time, but growing numbers were owners of licences in the rest of the shellfish industry for oysters, mussels and clams. Today the number of women directly holding licenses to fish is growing.

Even as the work of women fishers had increased and become more diverse, complex and multifaceted in the 1990s, it is fair to say that, even today, women in the fisheries are carrying a large share of the unpaid fisheries work and paid work which enables the families to survive financially.

Dianne on "setting day", the start of the lobster
season 2021 at Tignish Run, PEI

Over the past twenty years, more and more women hold their own lobster licences, owning, running, and maintaining, and have their own gear and fishing boats.

"As a wife of a fisherman and mother of three children, and while working alongside my husband," one woman wrote, "I sometimes feel that it is a thankless job. I need a voice to express my views as a wife, mother, labourer, and helpmate. I do know that I contribute a lot to our home & livelihood and to my spouse, but I would love a more active voice for myself." This woman had lived in a fishing family for more than twenty-one years.

The Government Reform process that began thirty years ago in 1990 still continues to impact the lives of women today. Globalization of the economy has made government leaner and some say — meaner. When services shift from the public sector to the community or directly to families, it is a form of privatization. This shift to individual responsibility, and the lack of definitive terms for the change has helped to confuse and obscure the government's reduction in the provision of services to citizens. This confusion leads to a debate about the value of women's work. Just like women's work in the fisheries, globalization has impacted women today. Women's work includes work at home, in paid work and in providing services to the family that were previously done by the government. We only need to consider healthcare to fully understand the dynamic taking place. More health care is being done at home with the help of family when a mother gave birth in a hospital she and her newborn stayed four or five days to rest, and to be supported in their care for themselves and their child. Today, women are lucky to get twenty-four hours of care before they are sent home as globalization and government reform have shifted responsibilities. I still believe that one of the major flaws of globalization is its negative impact on women — globalization has been a do-it-yourself movement. And that unpaid health care work is called the third sector, with paid work the first, unpaid fisheries work the second sector, and the unpaid former government services delegated to families as the third sector. Of course, while working in all three sectors women also bear responsibility for most of the care of the children at home, and they also continue to conduct much of the housework, in addition to their full time work. The question begs asking, "What has changed?"

CHAPTER FIVE:
WOMEN IN POLITICS

From the 1986 provincial election up until today, I have been a member of the Liberal Party, playing many different roles behind the scenes. When I was not involved directly in political campaigns, I was actively involved on the non-government side of the fence, lobbying the government for change. The richest, most varied, and most typical arena of women's political engagement is found in the politics of everyday life. The interactions between women, their governments, and political parties is enormous — but it is usually ignored as not 'real' politics. However, it is a large area of experience and influence, and this indirect form of political activity among women has been the norm in Prince Edward Island. There are concerns that women are being treated as unimportant citizens if they are not directly involved in governance, whether it be civic, provincial, or federal. As more and more women directly enter public life, the greater the opportunity for equality. However, the active involvement of volunteer party workers who are women have also made a significant impact on democracy. With equality, it is the hope of the many that policies will include a female perspective. Research shows that if women are one third of the group, they are perceived as the majority by the men, so the obvious solution to policy development is to involve more women.

We have very seldom reached the thirty percent level of involvement of women nominated to run in our provincial Legislature, so we continue to see women's activity in mostly a supportive, or secondary role inside political parties. The exception to this was when Premier Catherine Callbeck was in office and Marion Reid became Lieutenant Governor, Libbe Hubley became Deputy Speaker of the PEI Legislature and Nancy Guptill was the Speaker. Also, at that time, Pat Mella was the Leader of the Opposition and Leader of the Progressive Conservative Party. They became known as PEI's Famous Five.

For long term change to occur, political parties must not only make a concerted effort to seek female candidates, but furthermore provide campaign support. Only by making an intentional effort will equality in party elections become the norm. Without the direct participation of women in political parties, whether they are elected or they volunteer behind the scenes, democracy would be negatively affected. True democracy demands full participation of all citizens in choosing their governments.

The first political campaign where I was a member of the campaign committee was in 1986, when Shawn Murphy invited me to join the Sixth Queen's team to re-elect Paul Connolly and Joe Ghiz as MLAs. It was the election when Joe Ghiz first became the Premier. As a new campaign worker, I attended regular campaign meetings and worked to ensure students and other Island voters could vote by proxy. Because Joe Ghiz was the leader of the Liberal Party, he wanted to ensure we got as many supporters to vote as possible in the 1986 campaign.

His brother, Peter Ghiz was a law student at Dalhousie University at the time and we began the process to have his mother vote on his behalf. While she did complete the process, she neglected to get the forms to the returning officer on time. And I know now that I should have taken her there myself. Peter did vote in the election by coming home when his brother Joe insisted. Joe's opinion was, "If I lose by one vote, it won't be because my brother did not vote." With other parents of other students, I met late night flights carrying documents, we received registered mail and hand delivered forms from all around the district. From that campaign onward, and several times over the years, I sat on campaign committees in many roles at both the federal and provincial level.

While I enjoyed all aspects of politics, it was the work of advocacy that satisfied me the most, in my role as Chairperson of the Advisory

Council on the Status of Women and at the Women's Secretariat — even though they were difficult years for me. For me, there was a strict line between volunteering for the Party and working with women's groups where we hosted debates and prepared election guides for women voters and candidates. Although I was asked about helping out the Party, my answer during campaigns was no. Between campaigns it was the policy of the council to assist anyone looking to improve the status of women.

**Politican From Iceland
Addresses Women**

CHARLOTTETOWN — Gudrun Agnarsdottir (left), a member of the Women's Party in Iceland, talks with Dianne Porter, chairman of the P.E.I. Advisory Council on the Status of Women, following her speech at a fund raising dinner Wednesday evening. Agnarsdottir, a member of the Icelandic Parliament, talked of the importance of women entering the political system.

Meeting with Gudren Agnarsdottier, member of the
Women's Party, elected in Iceland

During one political leadership campaign, a woman candidate from the Progressive Conservative Party had her friend call me to discuss a number of women's issues. My advice was simple: if you want to be a Member of the Legislative Assembly, you have to look like a leader, sound like a leader, and you must give the speech of your life. I'm not sure if it made a big difference in her campaign, but it did change her understanding of campaigning. And when she added depth to her professional look, I was delighted to see when she won.

During the 1993 federal campaign, I was active doing some prep work by sitting in on mock debates to prepare the candidates on issues and style. The federal Liberal Party election document, *The Red Book* (officially titled *Creating Opportunity: The Liberal Plan for Canada*), was the basis of the 1993 federal campaign, and so my main activity for the campaigns became to teach male politicians about women's issues, and child care in particular. I was the campaign Co-Chair in one federal election with Gordon Campbell to elect George Proud and two provincial elections, one with Shawn Murphy to elect Jeannie Lea and the other to chair the campaign in District 14 in Charlottetown, where Dr. Barry Ling won the nomination. I firmly believed that if women were not active in these political campaigns, and actively preparing politicians and at planning tables behind the scenes, our issues would not become part of the candidate's campaign. It is and continues to be the job of women to push our own agendas, towards greater platforms of equality and balance. The best thing would be for women to become successful politicians; until then, greater numbers of women must be involved as part of the campaign teams and become active, trusted, and listened to because they have much experience to draw on.

During one federal campaign, I recruited a young group of new political activists to work with us in Hillsborough (the previous name for the Charlottetown federal riding), since I had noticed them while they were working together planning for the opening of the Confederation Bridge. Blake Johnson, Hans Connor, Laura Nicholson, Mary Nicholson, and Marla MacDonald joined the Hillsborough team and very keenly added much to our success. They stayed involved in the Liberal Party for many years as a dynamic group until their jobs and studies sent them off in other directions. Recruiting new members into the political process keeps democracy relevant to voters, with an urgency to include new and emerging ideas and issues. Women are a necessary part of the picture and recruitment of party candidates and volunteers is a challenge for every party.

One campaign I will never forget was that of MP George Proud, who had recently declared bankruptcy. He also had an outstanding loan from a city bootlegger and the media, eager to share updates, received a brown envelope informing them. I felt like I was dragging a dead horse at that point. Together, with a small group of senior campaign workers, Gordon Campbell and I worked out a public statement with George and gave it to *The Guardian*, which put the issue exclusively to rest. People knew and trusted George because in this honest statement, he did not try to deny his financial problem, created by a bad investment, nor did he deny having a loan from his good friend, the bootlegger. Honesty is always the best strategy, and because George Proud was honest, he won the day.

While George Proud was the MP for Hillsborough I was the Riding President. At our first meeting we spent some time talking about his philosophy. He truly cared about every person who walked through his door. He said, "Everyone who shows up here asking for help is having one of the worst days of their life, and I treat them honestly, kindly and with respect." While we did not agree on every policy issue, we respected each other's right to hold a different view.

Provincially, in the 1993 campaign when Catherine Callbeck ran to be Premier, Shawn Murphy and I co-chaired Jeannie Lea's campaign in Charlottetown. The women both worked very hard during the campaign and deserved their wins, much to the surprise of many in the community who felt that nominating women as candidates, and as leaders, was "risky business."

That election campaign proved that if women get nominated by political parties, they have the same chance as men did at winning. Premier Callbeck's leadership in the province was historical, and she became the first woman elected as a Premier in Canada.

Catherine Callbeck

My next campaign when I was the manager was during the year that elected Liberal Robert Ghiz as Leader of the Opposition. The candidate I worked with that year was Dr. Barry Ling, who was a neighbour in District fourteen where we both lived. We met for the first time to discuss strategy at his home. He was telling me how he wanted to present himself to the public: he declared that under no circumstances would he wear a tie or dress up in suits. I listened and then gave my opinions based on my campaign experience, but also informed him that men who wear ties had a ten percent advantage, and as the old adage went I gave him the option to start ten points behind; it was his choice. During the campaign, he did in the end choose to wear ties. In fact, he is fondly remembered for the big rallies he attended around the province, showing up in a red suit jacket and coordinating tie — complete with his big smile and the infectious laugh he was famous for.

During the election campaign, Barry had recorded a series of radio advertisements about the need to reform health care in the province. His main point was that the doctors had a significant role to play in the change of the system that was coming to correct developing issues like labour shortages. The ads ran on the radio for the first week and the Liberal campaign was on the rise, as were Barry's chances of winning, because the ads were popular. But things changed when a small delegation of medical doctors arrived at Barry's home for a late night courtesy call, telling him that his ads were dividing the profession at a time when they needed to be united. He was convinced to pull the ads for the good of the profession, in spite of the fact that the doctors who visited him were Progressive Conservatives. That was the emotional turning point of the campaign for him, and although the election results were close, Barry's campaign was lost.

At my first meeting with Catherine Callbeck, she was soon to become the candidate for the federal Member of Parliament in Malpeque. I was invited to her cottage in Fernwood to discuss women's issues. Lawyer Marlene Clark, one of her campaign workers, was also there taking notes and asking questions. After much discussion Catherine decided to visit every rural post office in her riding, where most of the postmasters were women and rural post offices were being threatened with closure across the Island. Women's jobs were at stake and Catherine cared deeply about them. My favourite *Guardian* photo of that campaign was of her standing with the sign-carrying, protesting postal workers and citizens of Victoria, PEI.

From time to time throughout Catherine's career in politics, I was called on to catch up on women's issues with her. I was one of many people she consulted with, so it was not unusual to be invited to have lunch together and discuss the possible leadership of the Liberal Party of PEI. For people who know her, they will tell you she is thorough. She asks questions until all the answers are clear from every conceivable angle. The secret to her lifelong success has been her attention to detail, her ability to reach out to many for their opinions, and to take advice from the people of this province that she cares deeply for. How Catherine lives and works is based on long-held principles of justice, fairness, and loyalty.

During the time that she was a Canadian Senator, we spoke often and I would brief her on issues of concern to women on the Island. I am always astounded at the scope of her interest and her action-oriented ideas for solutions to problems. If she believes strongly in something, she stands by her principles and acts after quiet deliberation; once all the facts are known.

For fifteen years I acted as the Policy Chairperson for the Malpeque Federal Liberal Riding Association Executive, when Wayne Easter was the Member of Parliament. There were federal policy conventions every second year, and PEI developed resolutions to take to the conventions for debate. For one national policy convention, the priority of the PEI Liberal resolution that was drafted in our riding was put forward to the national convention. It was supporting a basic income guarantee (BIG), to be worked out with the provinces. The resolution was strongly supported by the large policy convention in Montreal that year, and was enthusiastically passed by more than a thousand delegates. Not one delegate spoke out against it. As many know, party policy and government policy are two separate things. If a Liberal government chooses to ignore Liberal Party resolutions, they are given the freedom to do so.

The lobbying work must continue on many fronts after policy conventions, and a great commitment to active lobbying in particular. Even when the party supports the issue, the community must continue to lobby. Today, PEI has an active community organization working to implement a basic income program. At the present time, there does not appear to be sufficient political support from either the federal or provincial government. As a policy, I believe it will bring people out of poverty, like the Canadian Emergency Response Benefit (CERB) payments did during the COVID-19 pandemic in Canada in 2020-21.

Another political role I took on was as the PEI coordinator for MP Carolyn Bennett's campaign to become leader of the federal Liberal Party of Canada in 2006. We were a small enthusiastic group of supporters here on the Island and we held a well-attended rally in rural PEI, which included an energetic group of medical students who were transported from their convention at the Delta Hotel in a double-decker bus. Through negotiations mid-way in the campaign, Carolyn decided to support Bob Rae and as her potential delegates, we were expected to support him also. Some people followed her lead but others did not choose a candidate until the convention speeches were given. The battle lines were drawn between Rae and a new politician on the scene, Michael Ignatieff, who appeared to be the front runner. Many of us, however, sensed the need to go with someone with new ideas and on the last ballot the convention elected MP Stephane Dion, who came to the convention with his green signs, green T-shirts, and a green policy agenda. Some might say his policy agenda was ahead of its time, because shortly after his election as Leader his support started to wane. Some MPs and some Party insiders did not support him.

The discussion of sexism in politics is an extensive topic. On the Federal level, getting policy resolutions that were considered women's issues on the floor for a vote was generally difficult, and lots of lobbying had to be done ahead of time. Sending the right messenger to speak to the resolution was vital. When the resolution calling for a National Child Care Program was on the agenda, one of our Island Liberal delegates was a very obviously pregnant Michelle Harris Genge. She was approached to deliver a supporting speech on child care. She and I had worked on her speech in Shawn Murphy's office on Parliament Hill with one of his staff until we had crafted a message with the most likelihood to be heard. When Michelle spoke on the convention floor, the room became quiet and everyone listened intently. We were thrilled when the resolution passed and became part of the Liberal Party policy file.

While I was Vice President of the PEI Liberal Party, I kept a neutral role as part of the planning committee that eventually elected Premier Robert Ghiz. During the year leading up to the convention when I became Chair, the President had been unable to act, so as Vice President I ran the monthly Executive meetings. When Robert attended the first meeting as Leader, he sat down beside me and pointed to Sean Casey and said, "He is the next President of the Party." I was shocked to be so dismissed, but I accepted that he wanted a loyal person and I did not work on his leadership campaign. When that man became President, though, he asked if I would work across the province to revitalize the Liberal Women's Commission and I agreed that more women's voices needed to be heard — so I signed on to the project.

Following the election of Robert Ghiz as Premier, I was hopeful that women would have an ally in the Premier's office again. I had spoken with Robert and other influential Liberals about the role of women in Cabinet and the rule of three. Research shows that if there are just three women in a group of men they are perceived as a large group and are able to be influential on issues of concern. Robert appeared to agree that three would be the number. I felt confident.

At the first meeting of the Executive on the day of the Cabinet swearing in, I was shocked and disappointed when only two women's names made the cut. Feeling ignored and less respected because of both times I had been ignored, I resigned and have not been involved in the provincial side of the Liberal Party since that time. That is when I joined the Malpeque federal executive as policy Chairperson and stayed in that position until Wayne Easter stepped down as the Member of Parliament.

In 2007, I joined the PEI Coalition for Women in Government, a multi-partisan non-profit organization dedicated to advancing women's leadership in political, civic, and democratic life in Prince Edward Island. For ten years I worked closely with Kirstin Lund and the group who had located grant money from Status of Women Canada under their women and leadership program. As is the case with many non-profit projects, women in the paid positions are also responsible for finding the funds. Kirstin was gifted at finding the niches in programs to fit the Coalition's objectives.

The early objective of the Coalition was to conduct research, and to discover the attitudes towards women in government. It was confirmed that when women are recruited by political parties and win nominations, they had the same chance at winning a seat in the Legislature or the House of Commons as men did. The glaring problem was getting female candidates who were prepared to run for nominations. Unfortunately, in my experience with candidate search committees in the Liberal Party, my lone voice among the group of men could only offer limited influence. We needed more women to be at the tables where search committees are at work in order to recruit more women as nominees. Most importantly, the whole political party membership must be willing to recruit, nominate, and elect more women. This is the case for all political parties.

The Coalition worked with women directly by offering campaign schools; political workshops on campaigning methods, getting the nomination, fundraising, and making the decision to run. Many of those attendees did get nominations in several political parties and some won and served in government. Women still remain the main caretakers in their families and cannot envision themselves balancing home with the demands of public life, especially during campaigns. It is not seen as an easy path by the women and there needs to be concerted effort to recruit, to get campaign and family support, and to get financial support for them as candidates.

During the campaign for Jeannie Lea, we contacted some of her friends about helping with some of those home-based responsibilities. However, she was very fortunate that her extended family stepped up to take a more active role in caring for her children and preparing meals. Her spouse took on more responsibility as well. Having a supportive partner and family like she did is a key support that will allow more women to become politicians.

Women getting from the sidelines of politics into a direct active role has been closely followed and results are posted on the website by the Coalition and I am hopeful that more women will step up in the future. With the support and encouragement of their families and political parties, it is possible. Kirstin Lund did an excellent job as the promoter, founder, staff person, and fundraiser for the Coalition.

UNSUNG HERO
KIRSTIN LUND

I decided I was going to be a lawyer when I was twelve and didn't deviate from that plan until I was actually practicing law. I had the rare advantage to sample several kinds of law practice as an articled clerk, spending five months with the Supreme Court of PEI and another five with the Crown Attorney's Office before finishing my articles at Carr, Stevenson & MacKay in Charlottetown. At all three, the people were wonderful — invested in my learning, committed to providing me with unique work that helped me experience multiple aspects of a legal practice. 

After being called to the bar in 1995, I continued to practice law with Carr, Stevenson & MacKay and became a board member of several organizations serving clients experiencing family violence. I discovered very early in my career that what I loved most of all was helping clients figure out how to help themselves — not necessarily a good fit in a profession where the revenue typically comes from solving people's problems for them. During my articles, I was exposed to interest-based negotiation and mediation and was drawn to the idea of facilitating processes that support people to solve their own conflicts.

Innovation makes up the most dominant aspect of my personality and I was an entrepreneur from a young age. My earliest entrepreneurial memory is going door to door at age seven selling hand-picked forget-me-nots for five cents — and then right to the neighbourhood store for penny candy with the proceeds. I continued my enterprising ways over the course of my young life, and it made sense to me at age twenty-six to do it again. Though I loved the people I worked with, most of the work itself was missing elements of innovation and creativity that naturally called to me. Eighteen months into my legal career, when I was walking to lunch with one of the partners in my firm, I shared that if I could do anything, I would mediate and do work in the area of family violence prevention. And when I give voice to ideas, I tend to manifest them.

So, after two years of lawyering, I left the practice and opened a mediation firm, doing mostly family law mediation for couples going through divorce and training individuals and teams in effective conflict management and prevention, both through my business and at UPEI. My deep interest in preventing family violence was high and in my first year of business, I found funding to coordinate a project that looked at family mediation in the context of intimate partner violence. The opportunity to bring people together to gain insight and plan strategies for change fueled me, and, in addition to providing mediation and conflict management training, I continued to envision and coordinate projects I hoped would lead to change in the area of violence prevention and restorative justice. I used my mediation skills to facilitate partnerships between communities and government to identify innovative ways to prevent violence and find solutions to minimize the re-victimization of survivors of violence in the justice system. With Julie Devon Dodd, I eventually founded the not-for-profit Justice Options for Women and over the course of the next twenty years we wrote funding proposals that brought over $4 million of federal funding into Prince Edward Island to work on family violence prevention strategies. One of the most significant outcomes of this work for me was that it brought together my mediation, collaboration, and facilitation work with family violence prevention in the creation of a process called Circles of Safety and Support, which provided an opportunity for collaborative safety planning for women at high risk for violence after leaving an abusive relationship.

Throughout the course of this work, it became apparent that unless there was political will, the innovative strategies created by community and government partners would sit on a shelf. There was evidence, both local and abroad, that when women were in positions of political decision-making, more focus and funds were likely to be expended on issues that predominantly impact women and children. And so in 2003, I began to devote some of my social entrepreneurship efforts towards getting more women elected, bringing together a multi-partisan team of women with a desire to see the goal of electing more women realized for Prince Edward Island. Dianne Porter was the first to say yes and became the unofficial chairperson while I played a coordinator role in the PEI Coalition for Women in Government. Over the course of the next decade and a half, we accessed federal funding to identify and implement action strategies for getting more women elected including data research, campaign schools, recommendations and challenges to political parties to nominate more women, communication campaigns and education and support for women to take on greater leadership roles, whether elected or within their parties and communities.

There comes a time when all innovators move on from what they've created, and between 2014 and 2018 I began sharpening my focus to supporting effective management of interpersonal workplace conflict, gradually transitioning the work of Justice Options for Women and the PEI Coalition for Women in Government to other capable women. Collaboration has been the one constant in my work — whether facilitating collaborative processes in communities, families, and workplaces or teaching others to collaborate effectively. Using insight and learning from my first twenty years of collaborative work, I have spent the last several developing resources and training designed to support work teams and individuals to effectively manage conflict and create cultures of collaboration. I provide many of those resources, including worksheets, guides and a podcast, free of charge at collaborationschool.com.

In 2014, Canada was celebrating the 150th anniversary of the Charlottetown Conference. This meeting created a dream and the beginning of a conversation about what the country could be. It is known as a pivotal time, when British North American colonies took steps to create the dominion known as Canada. PEI 2014 Inc. announced a community grant fund inviting groups to develop projects to celebrate the 150 years. Brought together by the Coalition for Women in Government and other women's groups, and under Kirstin Lund's leadership, organizations took part in a discussion to develop a unique opportunity. The process was facilitated so women political leaders from across the country could develop a vision of what Canada would look like in the next 150 years if more women were involved as organizers and candidates. The book which reflects this project is called, *A Bold Vision: Women Leaders Imagining Canada's Future*, and it was published by Women's Network PEI and edited by Jane Ledwell from the Advisory Council on the Status of Women.

The Coalition is still actively promoting women to become candidates and over time has kept statistics on the outcomes of each campaign. There has never been a time where more than one third of the candidates in any election are women, even though women make up 50% of the population. There is still much work to do.

Behind the scenes volunteer work is where most political women operate across the Island; certainly this is the case within the Liberal Party, and I suspect the same is true for other parties. They raise funds, coordinate events, stuff envelopes for mail-outs, sit on executive committees and chair other committees, serve in executive positions, and run campaigns and offices for MLAs and MPs. On election day, they get on the phones to get voters out. There is a deep wealth of female election knowledge and experience on the Island that has been put to use for decades. This keeps our democracy alive and well. Between elections, the goal for these insiders is to maintain support for the elected MLA or MP, and dozens of Island women are active in the background of politics doing just that. It is time for the men of the parties to recognize the wealth of knowledge that exists and support women to come forward to seek nominations and become part of leadership in PEI politics.

I want to highlight two women whom I have volunteered with over the years: Eileen Doyle and Elayne MacLaine from Charlottetown, who have served on committees and in virtually every campaign role known to man. The Liberal Party has a Women's Commission who, in the early years, organized as a group to work for candidates and put women's policy resolutions forward at both the provincial and federal level conventions and during campaigns. Recently, although the Commission still exists, women have become more integrated into the provincial Party at all levels and are less involved in the Commission.

Liberal Women's Commission member Eileen Doyle, now ninety-three years old, has never missed an election campaign and she continues to sell tickets to raise funds. If there is a Liberal event in Charlottetown, you can be sure that she is at the welcome desk. In the mayoral race in Charlottetown in 2019, she coordinated a number of social teas in the city's seniors homes for Mayor Phillip Brown. She was ninety at the time.

While Lieutenant Governor Gilbert Clements was in office, followed by His Honour Leonce Bernard, Eileen was the official hostess at Fanningbank of many teas, lunches, and dinners and private events for their Honours and their spouses. All of this is volunteer work and is vital to the success of the office of the Lieutenant Governor.

Eileen Doyle, center, with His Honour, Lieutenant Governor Gilbert Clements and Her Honour Wilma Clements

Elayne MacLaine began to work in the Liberal Party in the 1960s and has never stopped. Just recently she worked for MP Sean Casey in the 2021 federal election campaign office. She is very active in the Liberal Women's Commission as well and has served as the PEI representative to the Federal Liberal Women's Commission for the past fifteen years. In that role, she also sits on the PEI provincial executive of the Liberal Party. At age seventy-five she is now recruiting for her replacement. In this photo with Catherine Callbeck, Elayne is presenting a Certificate of Recognition from the Liberal Women's Commission on the occasion of Catherine's eightieth birthday. Together, Eileen and Elayne have volunteered in Liberal politics for almost a century.

Elayne MacLaine presenting a Liberal Women's
Commission certificate recognizing Catherine Callbeck's
eightieth birthday

In the 2000 Provincial election, I was a candidate in Charlottetown. It was a contested nomination against a man I knew well, Joe MacDonald. When I won the nomination he began immediately to work towards getting my signage ready and his spouse, Anne Marie, worked in the campaign office and provided excellent information and communication with voters who called or stopped by. That is how we rolled in the District where I lived; we helped one another out no matter who was on the ticket. I was lucky and thankful that the very experienced Shawn Murphy was my campaign manager, Frank Zakem found very visible campaign office space, and a group of women and youth were campaign workers.

The internal polling was not at all favourable for any Liberal candidates in that 2000 election. However, we all worked hard and did our best to put the campaign policies front and centre. The door to door campaign was not difficult for me — as many people know, I have a gift of the gab. Throughout the riding, I met people from all walks of life and saw some concerning situations. It is times like that when the advocate in me came forward and I was able to connect people to organizations that could help them; the number for Anderson House, and contact with resources for community food supplies. I was aware that this may come up at the candidate training program put on by the Party after all the nominations were completed. On election day there was one Liberal standing, Ronnie MacKinley from Cornwall. While he was the lone Liberal in the legislature, many defeated candidates helped him out in the years ahead by chairing meetings on policy, attending conferences and poll meetings across the province on his behalf.

In January 2001, Carleton University asked if I would teach a senior year seminar on "Globalization and Social Change: The Impact on Women", so I was again headed off to Ottawa for the academic year. I enjoyed the classroom work and laughed when a couple of students referred to me as a hippie, likely because of my jeans and focus on peace issues. With good evaluations from the students, the Canadian Studies department offered me more teaching opportunities. As is the case with sessional lecturers, it is not a livable income so personal funds from other work was necessary.

Towards the end of the term, I began exploring teaching possibilities at UPEI so I could teach and live at home on the Island. The extension department was keen to have me repeat the same Globalization seminar on the Island. I added up the UPEI-specific time it took to prepare the course, place resources in the library, review and order the text books, and prepare handouts from journals to add to the course reading list. The extension department decided to cancel the course without consulting me or the students who were trying to register. Without student enrollment, there was no money to pay me for my prep-work, and I found this situation exploitative and manipulative. I never did get an answer as to why the course was cancelled. After discussions with other sessional lecturers I discovered it to be normal practice at UPEI at the time, so from then onward I did not apply to teach any course at the university. I can understand the frustration of many sessional lecturers with the lack of respect and low wages for the teaching that has become an exploitative, cheap part of many programs at the university.

Over the past twenty years, my volunteer work has varied. However, because of my interest in politics both local and global, I have followed issues here and in other parts of the world. Sometimes, I write opinion pieces. After visiting New York in 2001 at Ground Zero, I wrote a short piece called "There is a labyrinth at Ground Zero: A Chance to Begin Again." This is a draft letter that I wrote in the summer of 2021 while the Taliban was taking over Afghanistan and women's activities were being suppressed.

Dear Editor,

Literacy is the world's biggest peace issue and at this time many women and men across the world are clamouring to ensure the education of young girls in Afghanistan. It is an authoritarian State that has sponsored terrorism against the West. They supported the terrorists that bombed the Twin Towers in New York in 2001. They also repressed females and promoted male power in order to ensure a narrow world view. They were in control.

For so many in the world, books are accessible. However, the poor and illiterate find them a luxury. Illiteracy causes a continuous repetition of past failures which create the conditions for conflict. In Afghanistan, the Western democracies set out to support the education of girls and instead created a culture where hope emerged. The whole society benefited from the twenty year commitment to provide educational opportunities to all.

Today, I support the evacuation of the hopeful from the invading, rising terrorist forces. How can we bring Afghanistan out of another takeover by terrorists? How can the West create peace in a land that is reverting to the Middle Ages again? We cannot, we can only send support to the women of Afghanistan so they may speak for themselves.

For girls and women the chance for equality has been forcefully taken from them. Many must justifiably flee their homes and their country. They are in hiding.

It is my greatest hope that an avalanche of new books, written by Afghan women in exile, will illuminate their experience and create a vision for the future of their beautiful and frightening complex country. They know the path to equality because they have walked it and have experienced freedom for twenty years before the takeover by the Taliban. Women must write their stories for their own people and lead the way forward. There is hope. There is a chance to begin again.

Linda Gaudet, Ann Sherman and Dianne Hicks Morrow
attending the fundraising event in support of Afghanistan
Women, organized by Mo Duffy Cobb 2021

CHAPTER SIX: CARE TOO MUCH

Caring is part of my nature. Growing up in a large family, we learned to care for one another: for our pets, for our extended family, neighbours, and friends. At home we shared chores and did errands, and people along the road would call to request that I come help out when help was needed. Babysitting in the community was a natural occurrence. One time an expectant mother at her due date was going to be alone until her husband returned from work. It was actually quite scary to have such a big responsibility, to run home for help if the baby decided to show. I watched that mother like a hawk and thankfully her husband returned home at suppertime, with enough time to be there for the delivery with a local midwife.

During the time when I was lobbying for improvements for child care services on the Island one man said to me, "You know the problem with you, Dianne? It's that you care too much!" Perplexed, I wondered how you could *care too much*?

Shortly afterwards, I was asked to give the church service at Spring Park United Church one Sunday when Rev. Gary Clark was away and that opportunity gave me cause to reflect on the notion of caring.

In the context of an issue of the day, the closure of the CFB Summerside, I titled the sermon "Caring Too Much." I asked the congregation how could you care too much for Summerside, who was about to lose its main employer in town? Do we not care about those people, their children, the mortgages they hold or the bills to pay; and what about food for families who had formerly had jobs on the base? At the end of that talk I challenged the congregation to "care too much" about Summerside; to attend the march, scheduled for that afternoon, and to offer their time to help the community group fund a make-shift office for volunteers.

You see, by caring too much we lift people up, we stand with them, and we find ways to acquire what is needed to move an issue forward. It took many months for Summerside to receive the assurances of the federal government of financial support and some time later for the announcement of the relocation of the federal, Canada Revenue Agency's Tax Centre to Summerside. With provincial, federal and municipal governments and community volunteers working together over the long term, by "caring too much" solutions were being found and ordinary citizens ensured that pressure was kept on decision makers.

Whenever confronted with problems, my "caring gene" kicks in and I begin to focus on finding solutions, noting community concerns, the lack of child care, the lack of good paying jobs for women, and concerns for a friend or neighbour needing help.

It is natural for people to care deeply for family members, whether they are ill, afraid, short of funds, or lonely. We are encouraged from a young age to care for one another. In my family of origin, we cared for one another and now we all gather when someone is in need of support of any kind. Peter and I encouraged our children to be supporters of each other and now that they are adults they regularly talk on the phone, seek one another's opinions on problems, share items they no longer need, and plan their summer holidays together whenever they can.

My labyrinth focus began in 1997 while I was studying in Ottawa, when I became a member of a small women's book group. The labyrinth pattern has one concentric, circular path with no tricks or dead ends. Various styles of labyrinth patterns can be found in ancient cultures from all over the world, dating back as far as 5000 years. These archetypal patterns can be found in places as diverse as the south west of the United States where the Hopi people created a labyrinth called "the man in the maze". They have been found in Peru, Arizona, Iceland, Crete, Egypt, India,

Sweden, England, and France. There are hundreds of labyrinths globally still open for walking, both private and public, and I have travelled to many. They can be found using the World Wide Labyrinth Locator link on the www.Veriditas.org website. Veriditas is an organization whose purpose is to teach and share the labyrinth with the world so people may grow spiritually: to bring people together, to deepen compassion, to lessen judgement, to increase patience, and to find purpose. I believe we are all on the worldly path together and each one of us is unique.

Over the years of studying the labyrinth I have guided many people on labyrinth walks, in churches, at retreats, and conferences. There is a canvas labyrinth at Spring Park United Church which is painted and velcroed together to create a place for a walking meditation. Some call it a 'walking prayer'. Because of the nature of the work, many times walkers would speak with me afterwards and tell me their deepest thoughts or problems. I was conscious to not get in the way of their process, the awareness that was emerging or healing that was taking place. I did lots of reading about interpersonal communication and studied a course called Hakomi, a transpersonal psychology method developed by Dr. Ronald Kurtz. Over the three years of studying this practice part time, I was able to apply the methods to help the labyrinth walkers learn more about themselves.

During Peter's terminal illness from 2016-2018, he was able to stay at home and at the cottage most of the time, except if he developed a medical condition that required a few days in hospital. At the end of his life he had the expert advice and support from the Integrated Palliative Care Program, an excellent PEI health care program that links family, doctors, home care nurses, hospital, Cancer Treatment Centre, and Palliative Care. The communication and sharing of information made life easier in that all had access to the same information and recorded their treatments, medications, patient visits, referrals, and the involvement of spiritual care based at the QEH and Cancer Treatment Centre.

I am often asked how the system worked and if there are improvements that can be made. I can honestly say the system worked perfectly for Peter's needs. The family greatly admired all that was done to meet our needs as well.

The end of life care at home for Peter was a family matter. It was a very sad and complicated process of visits to hospitals for tests, treatments, and interventions when things would not go as expected. The home care nurse often briefed us on the next steps and was active in his care and, with her support, for the care that I provided.

One exceptional gift, a handmade quilt by our friend, Nancy Coffin, went with us wherever we happened to go; the cottage, the apartment, the treatment centre, the hospital, and even in the car. It was of great comfort to Peter during his illness. Peter thanked Nancy many times for her caring; not just for him, but for all that she was doing for the family. She drove visitors to the airport, babysat the young grandchildren, made meals, and brought treats at just the right time.

There were also many offers of caring and kindness from others in the community, for assisting me with moving Peter around the apartment, speaking with him candidly about this prognosis, neighbours bringing his favourite soup, and a few close friends who stopped by for short visits.

When walking through my life now, by the water, with a friend, through the woods at Bonshaw, or along the Confederation Trail, I remember how these small journeys are contemplative, like walking a labyrinth. As we walk the winding path of life, the unpredictability of the future is obvious.

For those who follow the Christian tradition, a reflection on Galatians 5:22-23: presents the labyrinth of life: "The fruit of the Spirit is love, joy, peace, patience, kindness, generosity, faithfulness, gentleness and self-control." Walk a labyrinth and express gratitude for your life and your journey. We can also take assurance from Samuel 22:33: "The God who has guided me with strength has opened wide my path."

In the Buddhist tradition, happiness is sought by following four basic tenets which are taught here on the Island. I first heard about this approach from the Buddhist nuns who spoke at a Senior's College class I was attending. OMAK is simply: Observe Merit and Appreciate Kindness. It urges us to seek the best in others and in situations and to be thankful for all kindnesses shown and given, whether to us individually or to a group we care about in our lives. When practised as a matter of routine optimism emerges and happiness becomes evident.

My labyrinth journey continues as a widow, mother, and grandmother.

The labyrinth of my life continues to reveal itself as I put one foot in front of the other day by day and I continue to meet others who are on their own journey on the path. The challenge for all of us is to care too much.

Labyrinth at Chartres, France

The Labyrinth Journey

To walk a labyrinth is to walk a sacred path. Every person does so at their own speed, in their own time and in their own way.

There is no right or wrong way. Trust the path to take you to the centre and back again.

At the beginning, pause, ask a question, say a prayer, or meditate to slow your thinking and become calm.

Travel at your own pace, let go, **Release** worries and concerns.

It is okay to pass others on the path by simply taking a side step without disturbing the other person.

We all travel our own way; there will be some leaving as we are entering the labyrinth.

At the centre, open your heart to **Receive** guidance, insight, an answer to a question or simply just be there.

When you feel ready, walk back out following the same path.

Return, think of how your answers or insights might be incorporated into your life.

When you leave the labyrinth **Reflect** and be grateful for the path.

Remember

Afterwords

My journey along this labyrinth life path began in childhood, where events and experiences laid the foundation for a life of empathy, service, and determination, and where I met many like-minded people, to collaborate and spend quality time with.

I have used the labyrinth as a symbol of transformation which reflects the changes I see in PEI society in the fifty years I have called PEI home, especially changes for women and children.

In this book, my aim has been to demonstrate that the history of Island women has been hidden and undervalued. It has been my intention to demonstrate the collective and collaborative nature of women's work and its value to our society. When added together, the unsung heroes who have written in this book from their own unique perspective create a tapestry which provides a glimpse into excellence, quality, dedication, and hope for the future. They leave a legacy, shoulders to stand on, for young people to understand and create a new starting place for generations to come, along this pathway to equality for Island women and children.

To all the unsung heroes who have contributed to this book, my very sincere appreciation.

To my children and grandchildren, I say a sincere thank you for always listening, debating, and bringing up the ideas from your generations which have given me such joy.

To Pownal Street Press, the publisher of this book, I say thank you for teaching me the process which authors must go through to get a book out for the public to read. I have learned and appreciated the time it took. To Maureen Duffy Cobb I say thank you for the excellent writing suggestions for this book, for the times in our coaching sessions where your insight has turned my narrative in a new direction or had me cling to and reinforce an idea. Mo is a positive, supportive, and encouraging coach who shares her valuable time. Thank you to Genevive Loughlin for her extensive experience in publishing, which enlightened me as a first time author, and for her management skills. Both women offer much to the publishing industry in Prince Edward Island.

Bibliography

Atkinson, Heather Doane and Eleanor Smith. *Land of My Fathers: Shelburne County Nova Scotia's Early Welsh Families.* Volume 1. Stonycroft Publishing, 1989.

Canadian Child Care Federation. *Interaction.* Self-published. 1990 Winter Edition. Ottawa.

Eichler, Margrit. *The Pro Family Movement: Are They For or Against Families.* Ontario Institute for Studies in Education, 1986.

Pierson, Ruth Roach and Marjorie Griffin Cohen. "Canadian Women's Issues Volume II: Bold Visions", *Twenty Five Years of Women's Activism in English Canada.* James Lorimer & Company, 1995.

Porter, Dianne. *2012 Reproductive Rights Time-line for PEI.* Private document shared with women at UPEI and with politicians, 2012.

Porter, Dianne. *Women in Fishing Households in Prince Edward Island-1998, A Thesis.* Carleton University, 1999.

Prince Edward Island Advisory Council on the Status of Women. *Diversity, Vitality and Change: A Three Year Report.* Charlottetown, 1988.

Prince Edward Island Advisory Council on the Status of Women. *"Issues Then, Issues Now," Some Historical Perspective on Women's Equality on PEI.* 2008.

Prince Edward Island Government. *Report of the Committee to Review the PEI Advisory Council on the Status of Women.* Charlottetown, 1987.

Prince Edward Island Government. *Report of the Task Force on Quality Management.* Charlottetown, 1991.

Prince Edward Island Government. Women's Secretariat, 1st Annual Report. Chalottetown, 1991.

Smith, Eleanor Robertson. *Alexander & Agnes Hogg and their Descendants.* Stonycroft Publishing, 1992.

Women's Network. *A Bold Vision: Women Leaders Imagining Canada's Future.* Women's Network Inc, 2014.

With a Masters of Arts in Canadian Studies, Dianne Porter was a Founding Member of the Canadian Child Care Federation and the first Executive Director of the P.E.I. Interministerial Women's Secretariat. Dianne's work in equality issues on Prince Edward Island has been monumental: she has worked on the front lines of early childcare reform as the President of the P.E.I. Coalition for Women in Government, as Chair of the PEI Advisory Council on the Status of Women and on issues pertaining to the prevention of violence against women.

A tireless defender and a passionate leader for change, Dianne has made it her life's work to improve the lives of women, both on the front lines and behind the scenes with countless other advisory roles. Dianne has worked as a lecturer in Gender Studies at Carleton University, and in leadership roles at Red River Community College and Holland College. Dianne lives in Charlottetown, Prince Edward Island.